MW00608637

DOGGONE TRAVEL +
ADVENTURE GUIDE

BEST DOG-FRIENDLY DESTINATIONS, HOTELS
+ MORE FOR YOU AND YOUR TRAVEL HOUND!

The Doggone Travel+Adventure Guide

Published by:
CityDog Magazine
Seattle, Wash.
206.762.0643; citydogmagazine.com

First Edition: May 2019

ISBN: 978-0-692-09589-8

Text © CityDog Magazine. All rights reserved.
Photography © CityDog Magazine and individual photographers. All rights reserved.

Editor-in-Chief: Brandie Ahlgren
Managing Editor: Rebecca Sanchez
Assistant Editor: Susan Henderson

Contributing Photographers: Julie Austin, Julie Clegg, Amelia Soper, Emily Rieman, Holly Cook, Jamie Pflughoeft, Teri Pieper, Tushna Lehman, Jen Flynn, Nichole Sears and Lindsay Baca.

Thank you to Travel Tacoma and Pierce County and Travel Portland for use of photography.

Cover photo by Julie Clegg.

Printed in Seattle, Wash. by Consolidated Press.

All rights reserved. No part of this book may be translated or reproduced in any form, except brief extracts by a reviewer for the purpose of a review, without written permission of the copyright owner.

Although every effort was made to ensure that the information was correct at the time of going to press, the publisher does not assume and hereby disclaims any liability to any party for any loss or damage caused by errors, omissions, or any potential travel disruption due to labor or financial difficulty, whether such errors or omissions result from negligence, accident or any other cause.

About CityDog Magazine

The Magazine

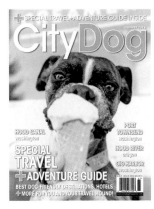

Launched in 2005, CityDog Magazine is the definitive dog lover's magazine about life and living with dogs in the Pacific Northwest. Published four times a year, each issue overflows with informative, insightful and often humorous articles on topics from cool canine products and the latest doggie trends, to regional activities for dogs and their people.

Our writers are dog people themselves, and craft articles aimed at engaging readers and generating excitement and action. We know that your interests are many and our editorial coverage is equally broad. Whether your purpose is sniffing out new places to visit with your best friend or digging up the latest from the local puparazzi, CityDog covers the canine beat.

Smart, city-savvy and fun, CityDog Magazine brings the joys of life with your four-legged friend to dog lovers throughout the Pacific Northwest. And, now you can start your own CityDog Magazine in your own city!

The Book

The Doggone Travel+Adventure Guide is a culmination of over 13 years of digging up the best places to sit, stay and play with your pooch in the Pacific Northwest. Our writers, editors and photographers have traveled throughout Washington and Oregon to find the best doggone getaways, the best dog-friendly hotels, and the best destinations for you and your travel hound, compiling all of it here, in this book, so you can start your adventures today!

The Website

CityDogMagazine.com is the go-to place to find all you need to know about living in the city you love with the four-legged love of your life; a place to discover some doggone great getaways, seek advice on health and behavior, search for pet-related businesses and services, find local dog-centric events, meet fellow dog lovers and shop for unique products for pooches and people.

The Editors

Over 13 years ago, Brandie Ahlgren, editor-in-chief of CityDog Magazine (pictured left; photo by Julie Austin), was introduced to a brand new universe when Scout, an eight-week-old boxer puppy entered her life. "I am proof of how a dog can change your life," she says. "I didn't grow up with dogs, so puppy parenting was new territory for me. I found most of my information came through word-of-mouth, which is fine, but a go-to resource with fresh, up-to-date content was missing in the Pacific Northwest." Hence, the concept for CityDog Magazine was born, and all these years later, is still going strong. Brandie resides in West Seattle with her dog, nine-year-old boxer, Thya, and can often be found hanging out at Westcrest dog park.

Managing editor Rebecca Sanchez lives in Seattle, Wash. with her three dogs and is a published author and nationally recognized leader in exploring the human-animal bond. Known as The Pet Lifestyle Guru, Rebecca firmly believes "we need animals as much as they need us!" To showcase her love of all things dog, Rebecca is the founder, chief creative officer, and brilliant mind behind the award-winning, social media star MattieDog, who happens to be 'A Little Dog Making A Big Impact In This World!'

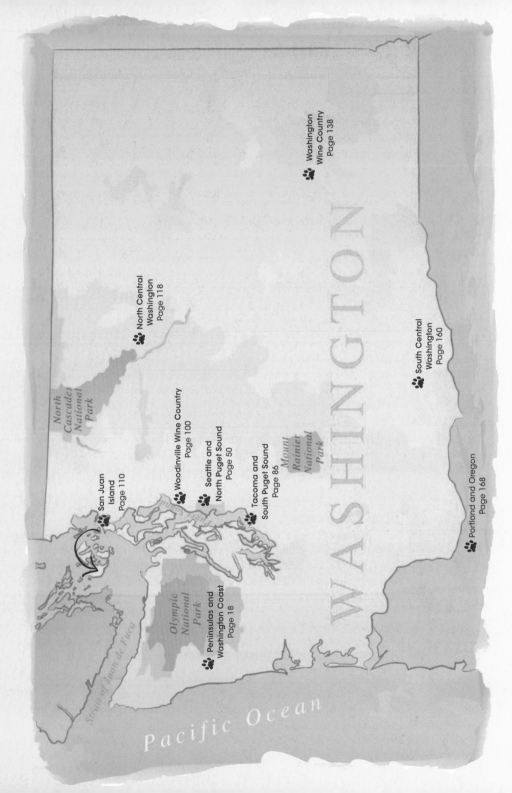

WASHINGTON

Washington
Wine Country
Page 138

North Central
Washington
Page 118

South Central
Washington
Page 160

North
Cascades
National
Park

Woodinville Wine Country
Page 100

Seattle and
North Puget Sound
Page 50

Tacoma and
South Puget Sound
Page 86

Mount
Rainier
National
Park

San Juan
Island
Page 110

Portland and Oregon
Page 168

Olympic
National
Park

Peninsulas and
Washington Coast
Page 18

Strait of Juan de Fuca

Pacific Ocean

Contents

Hit the Road with Rover

One can never be too prepared for a road trip with Rover, so here are some travel tips and gear for a comfortable, safe and of course, fun adventure.

Photo by Julie Austin

GET OUTSIDE & P.L.A.Y.
With these Go-to Outdoor Accessories

Use CITYDOG18
for 18% off.
While Supplies Last.

P.L.A.Y.
PET LIFESTYLE AND YOU

PetLifestyleAndYou

855.300.7529 | info@petplay.com | San Francisco, CA

www.PetPlay.com

THESE DAYS WHEN WE TAKE A VACATION, THE ENTIRE FAMILY ENJOYS THE GETAWAY, INCLUDING FURRY MEMBERS. ACCORDING TO A RECENT AMERICAN PET PRODUCT ASSOCIATION NATIONAL PET OWNERS SURVEY, NEARLY 40 PERCENT OF ALL DOG OWNERS TAKE THEIR PUPS ON TRIPS. ADDITIONALLY, ABOUT 10 PERCENT OF CAT OWNERS TOTE THEIR KITTY ON VACATION, TOO. PHOTOS BY JULIE AUSTIN

Traveling with pets is common over the summer, but the road isn't always easy going. There are a few things to consider before taking your pet on your next journey. To make sure you and your pup have a great trip, here are a few tips for your dog's health, wellness, and safety.

VISIT THE VET Pay a visit to your vet prior to traveling to help prevent your pet from getting sick. Talk with your vet to make sure your dog is healthy enough for travel, so that there are no surprises while you are on the road, potentially with limited access to medical resources. Explain your travel plans and explore flea and tick repellent as needed. Make sure your pet's vaccinations and boosters are current and ask about ones you may need for travel to help guarantee a safe and fun trip for both you and your furry friend. Anti-anxiety medication can help pets who are totally terrified of car rides and traveling, but begin the course about a month before departure. A healthy pet makes for the best travel buddy.

RESEARCH Proactively look up the specific rules in each state you plan to visit. It is important to be prepared, as each state has different rules and regulations. Some states require proof of vaccines and those vaccines may be different based on the state, while some states and cities may have breed restrictions.

IDENTIFICATION Update your dog's identification tag, attach it to his or her collar and keep it on the entire time they are traveling, even when just hanging out in the car. During your visit with the vet, make sure to have them scan your dog's microchip and double check that the information is up to date.

Clockwise from top: Protect your pet's paws with Ruffwear's all-terrain dog boots; never leave home without them—baggies, that is; be sure to pack the essentials including toys and treats.

TEACH WAIT The "wait" or "stay" command is a wonderful tool for getting out of the car. These commands can prevent your dog from bolting as soon as you open the car door. Simply tell your dog to "wait" and release them when you are ready.

TEACH TOUCH Every dog owner's nightmare is when the dog takes off. I'm sure we can all admit that we have let our dogs off the hook a few times when they didn't obey the "come" command. However, it's important to make sure to always have your dog under control while traveling. Try teaching him the "touch" command instead. This will teach him to touch your hand on cue in order to reset his recall. If your dog tries to run off and you say "touch," they are more likely to turn around and come back toward you. Treat rewards work wonders for the "touch" command.

LEASH AND HARNESS UP No matter how well behaved or trained your dog is, keep them on a leash. Better yet, a harnessed dog on a leash is more easily kept under control. When your dog is in a new,

unfamiliar environment he might not listen to you as well as he usually does. Also, remember that you don't know the other dogs or people in the area to trust your dog off-leash around them.

PRACTICE Take mini trips with your dog. Such as trips to the store, a park or just on drives around town. This will help your dog adapt to a car environment, and will also help them become more comfortable with staying in a car for longer periods of time. Additionally, it will give you an idea of how your dog will act in that setting, allowing you to avoid any surprises. Finally, practice provides you the opportunity to perfect your commands to make sure you and your furry friend are ready for a long distance trip.

FIRST-AID KIT You'll want to carry a pet first-aid kit in your car. You can either buy a kit specifically for pets or add pet-specific items to your own kit. Some things you should include are rubber gloves, hydrogen peroxide and a syringe to induce vomiting, self-adherent bandage tape like Vetwrap, gauze rolls, sterile pads, antiseptic towelettes, tongue depressor, eye wash, Benadryl, and a drying towel.

FOOD AND MEDICINE Travel is not the time to change your dog's food. Make sure you pack the food and treats your dog is accustomed to, and include your dog's bowl to help bring a bit of home to your travels. For dogs with specific nutritional needs, make sure to pack the necessary items. Also, if your dog requires medication, make sure that you have enough for the duration of your trip.

You'll also need to pay attention to the things that will make your adventure a calm and easy excursion. First is vehicle safety. The vast majority of et owners travel by car. Pets should never sit in the lap of the driver or front passenger seat. In some communities it is against the law. When a car stops abruptly, an unrestrained pet in the front or back seat becomes a projectile unless restrained by seat belts or a doggy car seat. You may want to consider a pet carrier for your dog. There are collars that emit calming pheromones for dogs that become anxious in pet carriers. Pets who get sick in the car may actually suffer from motion sickness. Mild cases might be handled with ginger cookies made for dogs. An animal or veterinary behavior consultant can provide a detailed program to help pets adjust to car rides that does not require drugs. Severe cases of car sickness may require veterinary medication. Lastly, to keep everyone happy while traveling in the car, make sure to pack some travel treats and water for both you and your dog.

Above: Wolfie enjoys West Paw's Montana Nap Dog Mat. Right: Walks are made easier with an On the Fly Jasper Swag Bag, with pockets and compartments for the essentials.

Finally, you'll want to understand if the campsite, inn, motel, or hotel that you and your pup are staying at allows pets. While times have changes and many overnight lodgings are pet friendly, according to AAA and Best Western International: of the pet owners who don't take their pets with them on vacation, more than 75 percent would change their minds if there were more pet-friendly places to stay. Many hotel or motel pet policies depend on the individual management's policy. When making a reservation, it's best to have your transaction done by email to help if you experience any issues. Some locations have weight and volume

restrictions where only pets under a certain number of pounds are welcome, as well as the number of pets per reservation. These are things you need to know in advance, not realize when you are fatigued and perhaps without many options. Likely, you will need to pay an extra fee or a refundable deposit for a pet stay.

Here at CityDog, we have a lot of experience traveling with pets. Throughout the years we've brought you stories that highlight some of the most interesting things you can do in the Pacific Northwest while out and about with your dog. We've also learned, through trial and error, about some of the best pet-related items that will help make travel with your dog a breeze. Here are our picks to help you become a seasoned adveture hound.

RECOMMENDED TRAVEL GEAR

PET SEAT Whether your canine travel companion is 10 pounds or 100 pounds, buckling up is a must. For petite pooches, we recommend the **Skybox Rear Booster Seat** from **Kurgo**. It is padded with low walls so it's comfy, cozy and gives just enough of a boost for little ones to peek into the front seat or see out the side window. The seat folds out in seconds, with a place to attach to your car's seatbelt and a tether to attach to your dog's harness.

Left: The Orvis Dog Traveler's Kit comes with two travel bowls to help keep Fido fed and hydrated. Above: Hattie sports an Insect Shield Dog Bandana to ward off mosquitos.

side pocket is a great place to stash a water bottle like the **Canine Canteen** (also by Orvis). It features a patented twist-top lid with a large-capacity drinking trough built right in to quickly quench your dog's thirst.

DOG BED FOR TRAVEL For a peaceful slumber, **Harry Barker's Toile Print Bedroll** combines style and comfort and comes with a matching strap for easy travel and storage. This dog bed is perfect for on-the-go travel with your adventure hound.

DOG BED FOR SNUGGLERS Some dogs seek comfort by snuggling, which can create a problem for travel. Nervous Nellies, here's your answer: **P.L.A.Y.'s Snuggle Bed** with dirt-resistant canvas on one side and luxurious faux fur on the other. This convertible burrow bed can be molded into a variety of shapes to match your dog's need for security and comfort, especially when away from home.

PET MATS To help keep your car clean try the **Montana Nap Dog Mat** by **West Paw**. It's light-weight so it travels easily, fitting perfectly in crates and the back seats of cars to keep upholstery clean and your pooch comfortable.

CAMPING BED For those dogs who like to 'ruff' it there's the **Highlands Bed** by **Ruffwear**. A packable, durable dog bed designed for comfort and insulation. Its lightweight synthetic insulation provides warmth and protection from hard, cold surfaces and compresses into a nifty stuff sack to attach to your backpack on hikes.

TRAVEL HARNESS The **Tru-Fit Smart Harness** by **Kurgo** is crash-tested and designed as a dog safety harness, not a converted walking harness. While the all-steel buckle system may seem a bit complicated at first, it is based on the engineering for harnesses used by rock climbers and has a carabiner to attach the harness to your car's seatbelt. Furthermore, the chest pad reduces stress on a dog's trachea and sternum while dispersing kinetic energy across the chest of the dog: important during those rare, but dangerous impact crashes.

DOG SEAT BELT LANYARD Designed to loop around any car seat belt system to secure your pet in the vehicle, **4Knines'** 20-inch, **Dog Seat Belt Lanyard** features a locking swivel carabiner for easy attachment. The swivel feature prevents your pet from getting twisted or caught up in the lanyard. Combine it with the **Everyday Harness** and you're ready to safely hit the road with your travel buddy.

TRAVEL BAGS We are in love with **Orvis' Dog Traveler's Kit** that features a rugged nylon canvas bag designed to pack all of your pooch's essentials. The smart design features three polypropylene-lined compartments and comes with a separate bag to store your dog's travel food and water bowls. Pockets in the lid are perfect for treats plus leashes, small towels, or other travel accessories and the mesh

DOG BACKPACK The **Baxter Pack** by **Kurgo** is perfect for everyday use or backpacking adventures. Built strong to withstand rugged outdoor conditions, it has eight different adjustment points for a proper fit and includes a rear-mounted leash hook that works like a harness for pups that need to be on a leash while on the trail. The ergonomic padded spine support contours to your dog's back for a comfortable fit and provides weight distribution for the two saddlebags to store all of your canine's essentials.

SWAG BAG The **Jasper Swag Bag** is one of the most convenient and unique dog walking bags we've seen in a long time. With lots of easy access pockets, you can stash your phone and keys in the front pocket for easy access, slide some treats in the flap pocket to reward your dog for good behavior, attach your **Chuck-It** to the built-in strap for easy transport, and store a water bottle in the side mesh pocket and a toy in the other. Best of all, quickly access a baggy from the built-in poop bag dispenser.

BACKPACK PET CARRY ALL If your little one prefers to be carried or has difficulty walking, the hands-free, vet-approved carrier by **K9 Sport Sack** is easy to use and comfortable for both you and your little buddy. It can carry any pup up to 23 inches long that weighs less than 30 pounds. The forward-facing dog backpack features adjustable straps for the perfect fit, whether on a long hike or simply running errands.

Above: Ruffwear's Dirtbag Seat Cover protects against dirt and dog hair. Right: Pearl takes a drink from Ruffwear's Bivy Bowl while resting on an Insect Shield's travel blankiet.

PEST CONTROL FOR HUMANS AND PUPS Keep warm and repel insects at the same time with **Insect Shield's Zip-Up Hoodie** and **Buff**. Insect Shield technology converts clothing and gear into effective, long-lasting protection from mosquitoes, ticks, ants, flies and chiggers, including those that can carry dangerous diseases such as Lyme, malaria, Zika and heartworm. Your pooch will appreciate the same protection from pesky bugs with Insect Shield's **Doggie Bandana**. They also offer super soft blankets, dog beds, car seat covers, and more.

AUTO CARGO PROTECTOR Protect your cargo area from dirt and dog hair with **Orvis' Quilted Microfiber Cargo Protector**. A non-slip backing keeps the protector in place, even when your dog jumps in and out of the vehicle. Streamlined handles wedge into the base of the fold-down backseat to ensure an even more secure fit.

AUTO SEAT COVER The **Ruffwear Dirtbag Seat Cover** is a durable, waterproof cover that shields vehicle seats from the remnants of dog adventures. The convertible design can be installed in a traditional or hammock configuration and maintains access to seatbelts. We also recommend **4Knines'** super-durable car seat covers and cargo liners. The company also offers dog seat belts, harnesses and travel beds, among other items, with a percentage of every sale going to animal advocacy groups.

Above: Gussy cools off in Ruffwear's Jet Stream cooling vest.

AUTO CLEAN UP After a summer of travel, your car will no doubt look like it's traveled a thousand miles, whether you've made a hundred trips to the dog park or trekked cross-country and back. For this there is a product that gives your transportation that "new car" look and smell. **Kurgo's Car Care Upholstery Cleaner** will wipe away the dirt, scuffs, and muddy paw prints. Combine that with their **Odor Eliminator** and remove stinky pet odors quickly and easily. Simply spray the air, rugs and upholstery around your pet and instantly enjoy the fresh scent of cucumber. Best of all, both products are toxic free.

MUDDY PAW CLEANER Turn any plastic soda bottle into a portable shower. The **Mud Dog Travel Shower** by **Kurgo** simply screws onto most plastic bottles to create a quick, convenient shower to clean off a playful puppy or muddy gear after a romp on the trail. It fits standard soda bottles from 16 ounces to two liters.

DOG TOYS **West Paw's Zogoflex** dog toys are designed for dogs with an intense play drive and love to be active on land, in the water, chasing, and fetching. They fly, bounce, float, and best of all re-cycle back into a new Zogoflex with West Paw's recycling program.

SOFT CHEW TOYS We love **Tall Tails' Fish Squeaker Toy** constructed of a plush-ribbed-polyester fabric, it will keep your fuzzy best friend occupied, while the soft yet durable fabric stands up to hours and hours of playtime.

COOLING VEST On hot, summer days, **Ruffwear's Jet Stream Cooling Vest** efficiently cools dogs through shading and evaporative cooling. The vest's light-weight spandex provides shade over the back, while the three-layer evaporative cooling chest panel disperses heat from the dog's core. To activate, simply soak the vest in water, wring it out, then zip on your dog, and go.

TRAVEL BOWL Speaking of water, keep your dog hydrated with **Ruffwear's** col-lapsible **Bivy Bowl**. It's ultra-light, with single-wall construction to keep the bowl simple and clean.

FIRST AID KIT The **Adventure Dog Series** medical kit has comprehensive first aid solutions to keep both you and your four-legged hiking buddy safe on all your adventures together. It features human and canine first aid essentials including an emergency blanket to treat shock and hy-pothermia, emergency cold pack to reduce swelling of sprains, irrigation syringe to ef-fectively clean wounds, a splinter picker/tick remover, bandages, and more.

To learn more about any of these prod-ucts, visit the Travel+Living section of our website at citydogmagazine.com and click on Travel Gear. 🐾

Looking for a better way to travel with your furry best friend?

4Knines® Seat Covers & Cargo Liners

www.4Knines.com

Every Dog is an Explorer

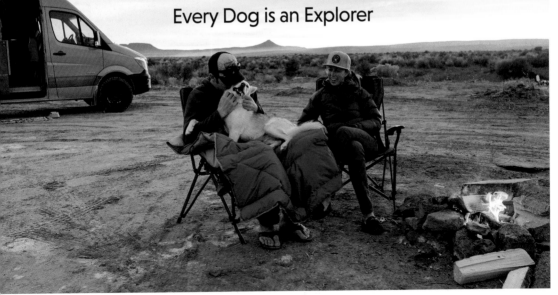

Peninsulas & Washington Coast

From the Olympic Peninsula to the Long Beach Peninsula, Washington's coastline is as diverse as it is dog friendly, with miles and miles of beaches for you and Rover to roam.

Photo by Julie Austin

ACTIVE CANINE NUTRITION

RUFF BAR
Dog Snacks

RUFF BAR®

Pure.
Natural.
Fresh.
Organic.

Fresh, organic,
natural ingredients
and our canine-centered
sensational recipe will provide
delicious nutrition for your companion
on the trail. Our RUFF BARs will fuel
performance on all your adventures and keep
your pup's tail wagging!

Available on Amazon,
in Mud Bay stores
and online!

ACTIVE CANINE NUTRITION

www.ruffbar.com   **f** Ruff-Bar-Dog-Snack   ⓘ ruff_bar

THE WASHINGTON COAST FEATURES ONE OF THE MOST DIVERSE COASTAL ENVIRONMENTS IN THE UNITED STATES. STARTING FROM THE NORTHWESTERN TIP OF THE OLYMPIC PENINSULA TO THE SOUTHERN EDGE OF THE LONG BEACH PENINSULA, WITH MILES OF BREATHTAKING BEAUTY IN BETWEEN.

Washington is home to many natural wonders, and for a glorious weekend or even a week or two make sure you explore the magical areas of the **Olympic**, **Kitsap** and **Long Beach Peninsulas** plus the **Washington Coast**—areas that are home to lush rainforests, a magnificent mountain range, and miles of coastline. This area of the Pacific Northwest is quite expansive, and you'll want to plan your trip, or even trips, accordingly. There is a lot to see and do, as this form of land is bordered by the Puget Sound to the east, the Pacific Ocean on the west, and North by the Strait of Juan de Fuca. In total, a landmass of nearly 4,000 miles.

This part of Washington state is home to rainforests, raging rivers, pristine lakes, and soaring mountains. The diversity of the area is both compelling and challenging, as you and your pup could spend a whole month exploring and never see the same thing twice. If you have the time, go for it! But like most people, you have to take it a weekend at a time, and that's why we've outlined a few itineraries for you to explore this natural wonderland. You can start your trip from just about any place, although we recommend packing up with some goodies and your fuzzy best friend and heading towards the Kitsap Peninsula area, then west through the Olympic National Forest, and traveling south along the coast toward Westport.

If time is of no concern, you can poke around the little towns in the area. Short on time? Make haste towards one of the larger towns such as Bremerton, Port Townsend or Long Beach and stay for a night or two—whatever your schedule, the peninsulas and coast are worth it!

Photo by Amelia Soper

HATTERS
GONNA HAT

New Mutt Hatter Toy Collection

Gladiator

Viking

Pirate

Leprechaun

Sheriff

Hidden squeaker & crinkles inside

www.PetPlay.com

855.300.7529 | info@petplay.com | San Francisco, CA

P.L.A.Y.
PET LIFESTYLE AND YOU

MAKE A SPLASH WITH THESE
SCOUT & ABOUT FAVORITES!

P.L.A.Y.
PET LIFESTYLE AND YOU

855.300.7529 | info@petplay.com | San Francisco, CA

www.PetPlay.com

Olympic Peninsula

WITH ITS INCREDIBLE RANGE OF PRECIPITATION AND ELEVATION, DIVERSITY IS THE HALLMARK OF OLYMPIC NATIONAL PARK.

Washington is home to many natural wonders, and the Olympic Peninsula is particularly special with its lush rainforests, magnificent mountain range, miles of coastline and of course, the 922,650-acre Olympic National Park. This International Biosphere Reserve and World Heritage Site is 95 percent wilderness, with just a handful of places to stay for people and pooches alike. We've discovered two such places for you to explore. Select one, or both for different nights, depending on the experience you want to enjoy.

STAY Located along the Sol Duc River, deep in the heart of the Olympic National Park, **Sol Duc Hot Springs Resort** offers a peaceful place to stroll, stretch, and soak. The resort's main attraction, Sol Duc Hot Springs, is a much-needed reprieve from a hectic life. Out here surrounded by beauty, you can turn off your cell phone and officially be off the grid. Which is a good thing since there is no cell phone service, landline, internet or television at Sol Duc, just the quiet sounds of nature and a very happy dog by your side as the two of you explore the serene surroundings.

Clockwise from top: Making our way to the main lodge at Lake Crescent; a couple enjoys a stroll along the dock at Lake Crescent; Thya and Ziggy enjoy the beautiful view; a pair of ducks 'taunt' Thya from the lake.

GETTING HERE Take Seattle-Bainbridge Ferry. Get on WA-3 N in Poulsbo, then WA-104 W and US-101 N through Port Angeles to Lake Crescent Rd or Sol Duc-Hot Springs Rd.

Photos by Emily Rieman

Left: Singer Tavern Cottages feature porches and rocking chairs to enjoy the view in comfort. Above: Thya explores one of many scenic trails at Lake Crescent Lodge.

the **Poolside Deli** nearby to provide hot and cold sandwiches with an espresso bar to aid you in your morning pick me up as you head out the door and continue your Olympic Peninsula journey.

STAY While the Sol Duc is the perfect place for relaxation and rejuvenation, if you and Rover are looking for a bit more modern conveniences with your recreation **Lake Crescent Lodge**, in the Olympic National Park, might just be the ticket. The Lodge, nestled among giant fir and hemlock trees on the shore of beautiful Lake Crescent, features the comfortable canine-friendly Singer Tavern Cottages. Built to resemble the property's original 1916 cottages, these charming little chalets featur lake and mountain views and are avail able with one or two bedroom arrange ments. All cottages are sans television to encourage relaxation, and come with a big comfortable bed, a full bathroom, and a cozy porch with wicker chairs that face the lake to take in the beautiful scenery.

Sol Duc was first discovered by settlers in the late 1880s and named after a Quileute word for "sparkling waters." According to Indian legend, the region was formed when two dragons battled for many years, scattering trees and boulders throughout the valley and shedding their skin to form the dense moss. After neither could defeat the other, each dragon retreated to its respective cave, crying hot tears that are the source for Sol Duc and Olympic hot springs.

PLAY Today, Sol Duc Hot Springs Resort features a mix of quaint, canine-friendly cabins, some with kitchens, some without, as well as three mineral hot spring pools and a large freshwater pool. The grounds and location of Sol Duc make it easy to leash up your pup and go outside and explore **Lover's Lane Loop**. A six mile round trip trek that meanders along the Sol Duc River, the Loop is an excellent way to stretch your legs and get your pup exercised before dinner, followed by a relaxing soak in the hot springs.

Meals are served at the **Springs Restaurant**, offering traditional lodge-like fare with a Pacific Northwest twist. Breakfast and lunch are available as well, and dinner hits it out of the park with a variety of salmon, chicken, and fish as well as their famous 'Build Your Own 100% Black Angus Cheeseburger.' If you get a little peckish while lounging by the pool, the Resort planned accordingly and positioned

Listed on the National Register of Historic Places, Lake Crescent Lodge maintains its turn-of-the-century charm but with some modern amenities sprinkled in such as free WiFi. In 1937, the Lodge was visited by President Franklin D. Roosevelt, who signed authorization for the creation of Olympic National Park in 1938. The main lodge is spacious, warm and inviting, with a huge fireplace and lots of comfy seating for you and your pup to snuggle up with a good book. Adjacent to the lobby s a large sunroom, with spectacular views of the lake, which makes for the perfect place for you and your dog to relax while you enjoy a glass of wine from the lodge's impressive wine list.

SIT The Lodge has a certified green restaurant that offers breakfast, lunch, and dinner from April through October, with a casual atmosphere, great food, and an award winning wine list comprised of Pacific Northwest selections. The menu is large and impressive, so you may want to sip on a Lake Crescent Mule, made with vodka, ginger beer, fresh lime juice and muddled mint, while you select your meal, from beer battered fish and chips, wild salmon, and roasted Pacific halibut, to a real treat, Dungeness crab spaghetti aglio e olio, made with parmigiana reggiano, olive oil, garlic, lemon zest, and crushed red pepper. To finish the meal, enjoy a slice of flourless chocolate cake with raspberry compote and whipped cream. Yum!

PLAY When you are ready for some exercise, the Lodge and its surrounding areas offer a lot of hikes. Not all trails are dog friendly, so be sure to check first where you and Fido are welcome. Our selection is the pooch welcoming, eight mile round trip **Spruce Railroad Trail**. You and your pup will enjoy walking the trail that snugs Crescent Lake along an old railroad bed. The line was once used to haul Sitka spruce trees out of the depths of the forest; hence, its namesake. Logged no more, the trail

No doubt, Lake Crescent is one of Washington's most beautiful destinations.

offers breathtaking scenery at every turn, with the main attraction about one mile in, where a large bridge spans a section of the lake and to the right you will see a gorgeous, still pool called the Punchbowl. This part of the hike is breathtaking, so stop and take some selfies with your pup. If you keep on hiking for another few miles you will be rewarded with views of Barnes Point and Mount Storm King. A little ways beyond leads you to the western trailhead, where you can rest up, have a snack and some water that you brought and when ready, turn around and head back to the Lodge. 🐾

Photo by Emily Rieman

PET-FRIENDLY PROPERTIES IN OLYMPIC NATIONAL PARK

Lake Crescent Lodge
416 Lake Crescent Road
Olympic National Park, Wash.

Rates start at $209 plus $25 pet fee.

Sol Duc Hot Springs Resort
12076 Sol Duc Hot Springs Road
Port Angeles, Wash.

Rates start at $210 plus $25 pet fee.

Lake Quinault Lodge
345 South Shore Road
Quinault, Wash.

Rates start at $117 plus $25 pet fee.

Log Cabin Resort
3183 East Beach Road
Port Angeles, Wash.

Rates start at $161 plus $25 pet fee.

Reservations: 866.297.7367 (all properties)

Season: Lake Quinault Lodge is open year-round, while Lake Crescent Lodge, Sol Duc Hot Springs Resort and Log Cabin Resort are closed during the winter. **Website:** olympicnationalparks.com

Port Townsend

QUINTESSENTIAL SMALL TOWN CHARM, PORT TOWNSEND IS A DOG LOVER'S DREAM.

Whether you take a ferry part way or drive there, Port Townsend is a must-see on every dog lover's list, particularly if you have a camper trailer. For those blessed with a road-traveling home-away-from-home, stay at the **Port of Port Townsend** marina and campground that offers RV sites with full hook up facilities, a laundromat and sparkling clean showers.

STAY Inside the campground is a small café for breakfast and lunch and a small, full-service restaurant with a deck that welcomes dogs. The view is spectacular from anywhere in the campground. No RV? Try **The Palace Hotel**, a three-story brick building constructed in 1889. Each room at The Palace has its own style, and your stay includes free WiFi, in-room refrigerators and microwaves, and tea and coffee service. The Palace is centrally located along downtown Port Townsend's waterfront area.

SIT However and wherever you decide to stay you must make haste to **Nifty Fiftys**, located in downtown Port Townsend. If you were a fan of the television show Happy Days, you'll swear Nifty Fiftys, a soda fountain shop from

Photos by Holly Cook

Clockwise from top: Mozi enjoys a romp at the beach; a bucket of lilacs adorns a table at Port of Port Townsend; deer are a frequent sight in Uptown; Chetzemoka Park is the perfect place for a picnic; Mozi drinks from a water fountain designed for dogs.

GETTING HERE Take the Edmonds - Kingston Ferry to Kingston then follow WA-104 W and WA-19 N to Discovery Road.

e 1950's, is where they got eir inspiration. Sit outside the dog-welcoming deck d enjoy a mushroom rger, or a kosher beef t dog, or maybe a grilled lmon salad or a basket of h and chips. Whatever u decide to eat, save room r a tasty ice cream sundae.

As you leave the diner, alk through the very small rden located right next or, and slip down to the each where you can hunt r sea glass while your dog atches the boats come and . After a brief respite, you d your pup can explore e downtown strip where inking fountains with igot heights that accom-odate adults, children and dogs n be found. In this part of Port wnsend you are able to find res of all types that showcase tiques, books, music, art, athletic ar, clothes, shoes, home and gar-n, gifts, and wine. Port Townsend fers a vast array of restaurants that fer a variety of food, snacks, cof-e, sweets and treats.

LAY Another great location to plore is the wharf where you and ur pooch can enjoy views of the ympic Mountain Range to the west d the Cascade Mountain Range the east, plus watch the ferries ug across the water, delivering ssengers from nearby Whidbey and. If you visit the wharf in the ening you'll be able to watch wntown Port Townsend light up the night time sky turns dark.

Nearing the end of the day, when ur pup needs to release any pent

A pair of pooches enjoy a romp on the beach at North Beach County Park.

up energy, head to **Chetzemoka Park** on the west side of town. Dogs on-leash are welcome, with many paths to wander offering access to the beach. At the park you'll find a small gazebo in the middle of the park and a garden of plants gifted to Port Townsend by the city of Vancouver, British Columbia. About 100 yards west of the park is a small, fully-fenced, off-leash dog park.

SIT If you want to get a late night bite before bed, try **Quench Waterfront Kitchen & Bar**. Quench offers a dog-friendly deck where you can get "a hint of Hawai'i and a taste of aloha!" with Pok'e and Hawaiian empanadas and other creative dishes.

Waking up rested, head to **Better Living Through Coffee** where you can shake off your case of the sleeps with fair-trade, organic, locally roast-ed drip coffee, espresso and lattes, and organic herbal teas and smoothies. Better Living also has fresh baked, delicious, nutrient-dense pastries, and quiches to fuel you for the busy day ahead.

Once fully pumped, you and your pup are ready to tackle the 503-acre **Fort Worden State Park**. Fort Worden originally provided the Puget Sound protection as a military base beginning in the late 1800's through 1973 when it became a state park. The fort features 100 historic buildings and sprawls two miles of the shorelines, offering views of the Olympic and Cascade Mountains, as well as the San Juan Islands. Fort Worden has a campus-like setting and it warmly welcomes people to learn and participate in a variety of arts, and woodworking, pottery and yoga classes,

Photo by Holly Cook

Photos by Holly Cook

Left: At Pippa's Real Tea, enjoy high tea with your pooch in their dog-friendly courtyard garden. **Above:** Mozi relaxes outside of Port Townsend Vineyards' tasting room.

MORE INFORMATION

Port of Port Townsend
2701 Jefferson Street
360.385.2828; portofpt.com

Rates: $43-$61, depending on season and location (regular hook up versus premium waterfront).

The Palace Hotel
1004 Water Street
palacehotelpt.com

Nifty Fiftys
817 Water Street
niftyfiftyspt.com

Quench Waterfront Kitche
1019 Water Street
quenchwaterfrontbar.com

Better Living Through Coffe
100 Tyler Street
bltcoffee.com

Fort Worden State Park
200 Battery Way
fortworden.org

Alchemy Bistro & Wine B
842 Washington Street
alchemybistroandwinebar.co

Courtyard Café
230 Quincy Street
courtyardcafept.com

Pippa's Real Tea
636 Water Street
pippasrealtea.com

For more information abou Port Townsend, visit their website at **enjoypt.com**.

a variety of conferences, music events, and camping and outdoor activities. Fort Worden also welcomes leashed, well-mannered dogs, and you can even enjoy a meal or libation at **Taps at Fort Worden**. If you have the day to spend here, we recommend a hike around the perimeter and through Artillery Hill before taking a stroll along the shoreline.

Back at downtown Port Townsend if you care to wet your whistle, try the adorable **Alchemy Bistro & Wine Bar** with a wonderful dog-friendly side patio. Alchemy creates divine dishes of sea scallops, oysters, mussels, prawns, frites, quesadillas, and pork belly. Don't leave Alchemy without sipping through the Sommelier's Muse wine flight. Or maybe you'd rather sit on a picnic table nestled under an apple tree in the patio area of **Courtyard Café**. At Courtyard you can enjoy a smooth cup of coffee along with a large, warm cinnamon roll covered in gooey icing, or perhaps a breakfast dish, or a hot or cold sandwich.

If you fancy a true tea experience you'll want to visit **Pippa's Real Tea** as advertised on their street sign that says "Come sit in our beautiful (dog friendly) courtyard garden!" To access the courtyard without going through the shop, follow the sidewalk a few doors down. It's small and hidden between buildings, where it leads to a wonderful garden, where you can sit at one of the patio tables and enjoy high tea with your canine. 🐾

Keeping Ball-Crazy Dogs Happy, Safe & Healthy Since 1999

A Real Ball Machine for Dogs

GoDogGoInc.com

Use code: CDSUM18 for $18 off

World's First Fetch Machine & Award Winning Automatic Ball Launcher for Dogs

Oceanfront Dog Friendly Rentals on Washington's Dog Friendliest Beach!!

www.vacationbythesea.com

360-268-1119

VACATION
by the sea

Kitsap Peninsula

JUST A HOP, SKIP AND FERRY RIDE AWAY, THE KITSAP PENINSULA IS YOUR GATEWAY TO FUN.

A short journey from Seattle aboard a Washington State ferry (or from West Seattle; directions below), the **Kitsap Peninsula**, commonly referred to as "the Kitsap," is surrounded by nearly 300 miles of shoreline with Port Orchard, Bremerton and Silverdale nestled in the center of it all. You'll find sophisticated dining, award-winning wineries, shops filled with local art and bakeries to tempt your taste buds. And, for your furry companions, quick access to pristine trails, waterfront boardwalks, and well-maintained on- and off-leash parks.

PLAY Take the 25-minute ferry ride from the Fauntleroy ferry dock in West Seattle to the Southworth ferry dock, located about 15 minutes from Port Orchard, where you will find fabulous acreage just waiting to be explored, starting with **Howe Farm**, a historic park with walking trails and an off-leash area. It's a favorite among local dog lovers and for good reason. Originally a working farm, the land was purchased by Kitsap County from Judy Howe in 1996. This 83-acre piece of property sits at the intersection of Mile Hill Drive and Long Lake Road and is nestled within a wide, gently sloping valley. It's doggie utopia at the off-leash park, that features

Clockwise from top: Enjoying the scenery at Evergreen Park; James enjoys a romp at Howe Farm; tasty treats at Naturally 4 Paws in Silverdale; the Kitsap Peninsula is just a short ferry ride away; James makes new friends at Howe Farm in Port Orchard.

Photos by Julie Clegg

GETTING HERE Follow Fauntleroy Way SW to the Southworth-Fauntleroy Ferry Terminal. Take the ferry to Southworth. Continue on WA-160 W to Port Orchard. Take WA-16 W to Bremerton or continue north on WA-3 to Silverdale.

1-acres of fenced area, including 5.5-acres of open space, and a series of paths winding through the woodlands. You can spend hours strolling around the idyllic grounds of the Farm.

IT When hunger bites, stop t **Carter & Company**, located on Bay Street in the heart of downtown Port Orchard. The bakery offers tasty coffee, and is filled with a variety of delectable goodies including breads, chocolates, and pastries like tarts, cinnamon rolls, Morning Glory muffins and a special scone of the day. If you truly feel indulgent go with our favorite, a maple bacon fritter. There are outdoor seats at Carter's where you and your dog can sit, eat your goodies and people watch. If you'd rather take your treats and head to the water, simply walk around the corner where you'll find **Marina Park**, with a boardwalk and covered gazebo. It offers beach access and is the site of a summertime, outdoor farmers market, where dogs are welcome.

PLAY After a small break, it's time to take the quick 15-minute drive to Bremerton. The largest city on the Kitsap Peninsula, Bremerton is surrounded by shoreline and home to the Puget Sound Naval Shipyard and the Bremerton annex of the Naval Base Kitsap, together comprising the third largest Naval base in the United States. Make **Harborside Fountain Park** your first stop. Located on the waterfront, the 2.5-acre park features five large copper-ringed fountains, wading pools, and lush

James explores Port Orchard Marina, backdropped by views of Bremerton.

landscaping. The boardwalk along the water is a favorite for walking dogs and taking in the views that overlook the marina and the Bremerton ferry dock. A new fountain park sits just above the Bremerton ferry tunnel and blends water and art, along with the bow of a ship and the conning tower of a submarine as a tribute to the Bremerton Naval Shipyard workers.

After taking in the scenery along Bremerton's waterfront, it's time to head to **Evergreen Park**, one of the prettiest parks on the peninsula. Comprised of 10 acres, the park features 1,900 feet of shoreline, a boat launch, picnic tables, a playground and plenty of parking. There is wide open green space for play time and a paved path meanders along the waterfront. If you happen to travel during the week, every Thursday during summer months the **Bremerton Farmers Market** hosts a variety of vendors offering everything from ice cream to handmade arts and crafts. Located nearby is **CJ's Evergreen General Store** if you want to pick up groceries or made from scratch meals or soups to go. Pull up a stool outside of CJ's and enjoy one of their tasty ice cream cones. Go ahead, share a bit with your pup, we won't tell!

Next, it's off to Silverdale, located eight miles north of Bremerton. Silverdale is a shopper's paradise, with the Kitsap Mall and **Naturally 4 Paws**, Kitsap County's only pet store to provide all-natural pet foods and treats, unique accessories and supplies, complete line of supplements, canine training center, full service grooming, certified animal massage therapy, self-service bathing stations, customer loyalty program and a Happy Birthday Club all under one roof. Naturally 4 Paws training and events center

Photo by Julie Clegg

Photos by Julie Clegg

Left: James and his person enjoy the overlook at Port Ochard Marina. Above: A selection of healthy treats at Naturally 4 Paws in Silverdale. Next page: Off-leash at Howe Farm.

PORT ORCHARD

Howe Farm
Take Hwy 16 to Sedgwick. Travel east on Sedgwick about three miles to Long Lake Road. Howe Farm is located on Long Lake Road between Mile Hill Drive and Sedgwick.

Carter & Company
707 Bay Street
carterandco.biz

Marina Park
707 Sidney Pkwy
portofbremerton.org

BREMERTON

Harborside Fountain Park
251 1st Street, Bremerton
bremertonwa.gov

Evergreen Rotarty Park
and **Farmers Market**
1500 Park Ave., Bremerton
www.ci.bremerton.wa.us

CJ's Evergreen General Store
1417 Park Ave., Bremerton
cjgeneralstore.weebly.com

SILVERDALE

Naturally 4 Paws
9337 Silverdale Way NW
naturally4paws.com

Silverdale Dog Park
11601 Silverdale Way NW
silverdaledogpark.org

Clear Creek Trail
9641 Levin Road
clearcreektrail.org

Silverdale Beach Hotel
3073 NW Bucklin Hill Road
Phone: 360.698.1000
silverdalebeachhotel.com

employs positive reinforcement methods and dogs seem to feel the family vibe as they learn their lessons in a room adorned with a wall mural depicting past and present pets of the store owners and friends.

While in Silverdale, don't miss **Old Town Silverdale**, a friendly community perched on the waterfront. You'll discover plenty of quaint shops, galleries and casual cafés with panoramic waterfront views. The waterfront park has a gazebo, playground for kids, public boat ramp, moorage, picnic spots, restaurants and a beach walkway. Another favorite is the scenic **Clear Creek Trail**, which winds through Silverdale's urban areas. Adjacent to the trail is the **Silverdale Dog Park**. The park is well maintained with a path leading into a large open area for some off-leash fun.

STAY If you're traveling for the day, then head back to Seattle via the Bremerton ferry. If you plan to stay for the night check out the dog-friendly **Best Western Plus Silverdale Beach Hotel**.

With waterfront views, the Silverdale Beach Hotel offers an indoor hot tub and swimming pool with floor-to-ceiling windows that overlook the beach, a sauna, fitness center, waterfront outdoor patio with fire pit, a beachfront martini lounge, and a deluxe breakfast buffet served daily. Not to mention the rooms have amazing views, and offer free WiFi, large TV, refrigerator, microwave, coffee maker, toiletries, and a hair blow dryer. A perfect location in a perfect waterfront town. 🐾

Hood Canal

EXPLORE WASHINGTON'S WILD SIDE, WITH STUNNING VIEWS OF THE OLYMPIC MOUNTAINS.

A trip around the west side of Washington wouldn't be complete without fetching your paws on **Hood Canal**. A completely natural waterway, the Hood Canal is a fjord along the west side of the Kitsap Peninsula. Filled with wonderous, natural sites and luxurious places to stay, it's as stunning as it is peaceful.

STAY **Alderbrook Resort & Spa** offers dog-loving travelers a reprieve from their road travels. Established in 1913, the resort is rich in Northwest history and in those days, no roads existed so visitors arrived by boat. Today, you can still arrive by boat, or seaplane if you're so inclined, at the lodge's full-service marina or simply hop on the ferry from Seattle to Bremerton or Fauntleroy to Southworth and drive an hour to the area.

Alderbrook offers 10 pet-friendly rooms and two pet-friendly cottages. All of the rooms feature stunning views of Hood Canal plus amenities for two- and four-legged alike including oversized soaking tubs, luxurious linens—including a custom Pendleton blanket—plush bathrobes with slippers, aromatic Molton Brown bath amenities, Keurig single cup coffee and tea selections and complimentary WiFi. Not to be

Clockwise from top: Beach combing at Twanoh State Park; relaxing in the warm and inviting lobby at Alderbrook; a ferry ride to the Kitsap Peninsula is part of the fun; a whimsical touch for a boat that has seen better days.

Photos by Julie Austin

GETTING HERE Take the Bremerton Ferry in downtown Seattle. Continue on W SR 304 to WA-3 towards Shelton. Continue on WA-3 through Belfair to WA-106, west towards Twanoh State Park. Alderbrook is 13 miles ahead on the right-hand side.

ft out, four-legged guests njoy goodies like a plush oy and treats. In addition to ne above, the resort's dog-riendly cottages feature ne and two bedrooms, a illy-furnished kitchen, eparate living room and ozy fireplace to curl up with your furry friend.

During your visit take me to tour the 54-foot ady **Alderbrook**. Without our dog, you can enjoy ne scenic sunset cruises hroughout the summer, nd hot cocoa cruises in December with Santa. You an also reserve the Lady Alderbrook for a private og-friendly cruise, but doesn't come cheap

It's easy to relax, and take in the stunning views at Alderbrook Lodge.

t approximately $500 an hour for a ninimum of two hours. However, the esort offers other low cost opportunities o enjoy the water including kayak nd stand-up paddle board rentals, sea ycles, hydrobikes, pedal boats, snorkel oards, floating tubes, a pontoon party oat, electric duffy boat, and open skiff with an outboard motor. They even ave doggie life vests if you accidentally eave your pup's at home.

IT Alderbrook's dining experience in-ludes a full-service restaurant and bar pecializing in locally harvested seafood rom Puget Sound and Hood Canal. he **Restaurant at Alderbrook** features special shore-to-table menu allowing uests to taste fresh ingredients sourced rom the region in a relaxed, yet elegant nvironment. The seasonal-driven menu xtends beyond seafood to focus on a ariety of ingredients foraged directly rom the ground's edible landscape. ach dish artfully pairs with Alder-

brook's robust selection of beer, wine, spirits and hard cider from the region. During the warmer months, guests can also dine al fresco with leashed Fido at one of the outdoor fire pits or at the **Patio Café**, which features a selection of more casual menu items like burgers and fish and chips plus live music.

Your visit to Alderbrook would not be complete without a spa treat-ment. Whether a signature massage, skin radiance facial or full-body treatment, the **Spa at Alderbrook** offers a range of holistic services alongside a full fitness center, steam room, dry sauna and outdoor pa-tio, where even pooches can enjoy a rejuvenating massage. If this isn't enough, connected to the Spa is a glass-enclosed, heated saltwater pool and hot tub with views of Hood Canal and the Olympics.

Make time to get out and explore the grounds of the resort. Conve-niently located next to the dog-friendly rooms, is a large, grassy lawn complete with a doggie waste station for potty breaks. The lawn is big enough to play a game of fetch with your pooch or a friendly game of badminton, volleyball, bocce ball or croquet with friends. Or, simply roast s'mores and enjoy the sunset at any one of the outdoor fire pits.

PLAY For a more strenuous activity, Alderbrook features over five miles of walking and hiking trails, making the resort a top destination for dog-loving outdoor enthusiasts. From an adventurous **Big Tree Loop** trail to the longer **Huckleberry Hillclimb** trail, there is a route for every age and skill level. Continue your doggone adventure along

Photo by Julie Austin

Photos by Julie Austin

Left: Alderbrook encourages guests to explore their artistic side, even the littlest ones. Above: Strolling along the dock at the Alderbrook Waterfront Center.

meandering boardwalks on **Licorice Fern** and marvel at the Pacific Northwest rain forest along the aptly-named **Dogwood Ridge**. There are enough trails, greenery, and views, that you and Fido will be out for hours. While it feels a world away, the good news is that you can't get lost as you'll circle back to Alderbrook Lodge.

For golf enthusiasts, Alderbrook features one of the most scenic golf courses in Washington. Open year round, the par 72 course offers rolling fairways bordered by massive evergreen trees and spectacular views. Even for non-golfers, the course offers plenty of fun, with a full-service restaurant and bar in the **Clubhouse** and a community park with tennis, bocce and pickle ball courts.

Venturing off property, nearby **Union City Market**, in the little town of Union, offers local art, unique gifts and gourmet food including monthly Canal Cookouts with Alderbrook executive chef Josh Delgado. Inquire at the front desk in the summer months for shuttle and water taxi service or if you have your car, it's just two miles up the road from the lodge. While there, be sure to visit **Cameo Boutique & Wine Shop**, located near Union City Market. Established in 1983, owner, Pam Hanson has created a unique shopping experience featuring fashions, jewelry, Pacific Northwest gourmet foods, wine, gifts and fine furnishings for your home.

SIT Union is great for exploring. This charming community is recognized as the first arts colony in Washington State, founded in the 1920s by Tacoma artist Orre Nobles. You can feel the region's artistic vibe, especially at places like **Robin Hood**

Village, Restaurant & Pub Situated on 15-acres, the Village is a well-known venue for local musicians who perform regularly at the weekly open mic sessions. The restaurant is famous for its creekside dining, woodsy ambiance and Pacific Northwest food which features a selection of regional and seasonal dishes in addition to an organic menu of locally grown products.

For more locally grown products, swing into **Hunter Farms**. Family owned and operated since 1889, the farm operates year-round, offering different "crops" depending on the season. Founded in 1984 by locals Karl and Bev Black, it's totally worth the indulgence, and in the summer months, or any month, don't resist a scoop of their Olympic Mountain Ice Cream. Hunter Farms also offers an array of house-made salsas, pickles, stuffed olives, sauces and preserves in its general store. During fall and winter, pick up a pumpkin from the pumpkin patch or a Christmas tree and wreath fresh from the Hunter's tree farm.

PLAY If you and Fido want to really stretch your legs, head to **Twanoh State Park** a 188-acre, marine camping park with 3,167 feet of saltwater shoreline on Hood Canal. It's the perfect

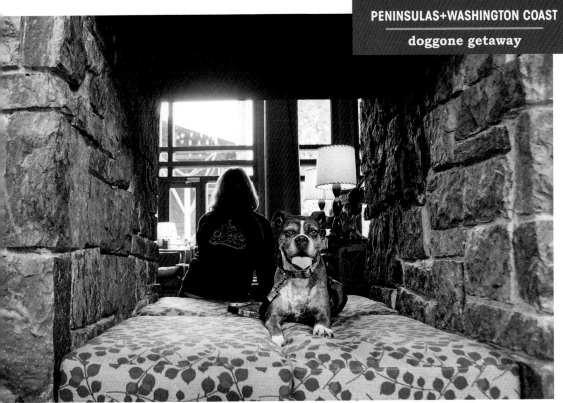

...hya finds a cozy nook next to the fireplace in the Alderbrook lobby.

...lace for a picnic or dip in the canal. ...t low tide, walk the beach with ...ido, keeping an eye out for orange ...ea stars, purple crabs and other ...ntertidal creatures. With a shellfish ...cense, you can even harvest your ...wn oysters for an afternoon snack ...resh from the sea.

With the Olympic Mountains so ...lose, don't miss the chance for a ...ike at **Staircase** or **Mount Ellinor** ...n the Olympic National Park. ...taircase is located in the south-...astern corner of the park, with ...everal short day hikes that have ...ou exploring the area. Shady Lane ...rail is flat, and less than a mile to ...ake Cushman. The hike to Flapjack ...akes is for the stronger hikers,

gaining over 3,000 feet in elevation. Mount Ellinor also gives you two trails to choose from. The lower trailhead at 2,600 feet welcomes you to the ascent with an easy grade at the outset. The route from the upper trailhead at 3,500 feet starts out with an immediate upward climb.

With boating, hiking, shopping, noshing, spa treatments, wine tasting, paddle boarding, swimming, and beach combing waiting for you and your pooch, a visit to Hood Canal must rank high on your places to sit, stay and play. 🐾

MORE INFORMATION

Alderbrook Resort & Spa
10 East Alderbrook Drive, Union
360.898.2200; alderbrookresort.com

Cameo Boutique & Wine Shop
6871 E State Route 106, Union, WA
360.898.3200; cameoboutique.com

Hunter Farms
1921 E State Route 106, Union
360.898.2222; hunter-farms.com

Robin Hood Village
6780 E State Route 106, Union
robinhoodvillageresort.com

Twanoh State Park
12190 E State Route 106, Union
parks.wa.gov/parks

Union City Market
5101 E State Route 106, Union, WA
360.898.3500; unioncitymarket.com

Photo by Julie Austin

Westport

WESTPORT IS WHERE IT'S AT IF YOU WANT TO CATCH A WAVE WITH YOUR COWABUNGA CANINE.

Surfing has gone to the dogs and nowhere is this more true than in Westport. Westport's main attraction for visitors is sport fishing, but it's also a popular destination among surfers, especially among surfers who love dogs. Why? Because, not only are the waves off Westport ideal for riding, but the town itself caters to canine companions.

PLAY Local businesses are dedicated to welcoming dog loving surfers more than ever before and with a seemingly endless expanse of sandy beaches, where leashes are optional, and the **Harold Hardy Trail** running parallel to the shore, which recently increased it number of pet stations to wash the sand from your dog's paws, it's easy to understand why Westport claims to be the dog friendliest beach in Washington State.

SIT There are numerous dog-friendly places to eat in Westport, and you can't go wrong with any selection. Our recommendation for a really good meal in a fun, dog-centric environment is The **Mermaid Deli & Pub**. Well-behaved dogs are welcome at the Mermaid, and are encouraged to roam the enclosed backyard while their people, seated in the outdoor picnic tables, indulge in a

Photos by Emily Rieman

Clockwise from top: Gus and Brenda check out surf conditions at Westhaven State Park; George hangs out while his person waxes a board; it's a howling good time hanging out at the beach; watching the waves; signage to stay safe at Westhaven State Park.

GETTING HERE From Seattle, follow I-5 S. Use right two lanes to take exit 104 for US-101. Follow US-101 for about five miles. Keep left to continue on WA-8 W, then US-12 W for approximately another 40 miles. Take WA-105 S to Montesano St S in Westport.

int of beer. For rainy days ere is heated, covered atio area to keep diners nd their dogs warm and ry. The Mermaid boasts e best hoagie in town, ccompanied by tasty icro-brews, and has laid aim to the favorite pub of e Washington coast. With eir very own Maui pork andwich made from oven-asted tenderloin topped ith honey-teriyaki sauce, matoes, red onions, and elted pepper jack cheese, e agree with their claim fame. Even their clam howder has us hankering return to the Mermaid.

Nelson has found a place to play behind the Mermaid Deli & Pub in Westport.

LAY With a good meal nder your belt, and our pup's needs all catered to, it's time explore Westport's beauty. Start with e **Westport Trail & Beach**, a nearby ree-mile paved trail heading out near e marina, just a few blocks north of the Mermaid. This trail, while short, offers a t to take in with sandy beaches and ocean iews everywhere. Your dog's nose will e sniffing the whole time. If you feel like oing for a little drive, pack up Rover and ead to **Westport Light State Park**. Just ash up your pup and explore the historic ghthouse and the numerous grounds and each areas. It's easy to spend a full day tak-ng in the scenery.

STAY Pet-friendly accommodations abound Westport, starting with the **Islander Motel**, eaturing dog-friendly rooms, many with a iew of the marina. Also, the newly-opened Westport Marina Cottages**, where you and our pooch can explore the docks at the marina or the beaches of Half Moon Bay. r, there is **Glenacres Historic Inn**, which oasts several dog-friendly rooms and cute

cottages. They also have a generous green space for Rover to run and a big fire pit, where you and your surf buddies can sit around a campfire and share stories about the day's best waves.

Another place that wholeheartedly throws out the welcome mat for Fido and friends is **Vacations by the Sea**, one of our favorite, dog friendliest, and most beautiful places to stay in all of Westport. Conveniently located at the head of the Harold Hardy Trail, the condominiums at Vacations by the Sea offer a plethora of amenities for humans. There is a putting green, seasonal heated pool, and year-round Jacuzzi. Dogs are given a treat upon arrival, or any time you stop by the clubhouse. The fully furnished, two-bedroom, two-bath condos are available to rent for a night, a few days, and even longer. Secure a condo that overlooks the ocean, with a fantastic deck where the dogs can check out the action while you enjoy the view. If you absolutely love the area, Vacations by the Sea has condos available to purchase for your own personal getaway.

At Vacations by the Sea, there is easy access to the beach to let the dogs run, search for sand dollars, and check out the sunset. Be sure to watch the surfing that happens at **Westhaven State Park**. A nice walk with your dog down the paved Harold Hardy Trail or a short drive with your surfboards, Westhaven State Park features 1,215 feet of shoreline on the Pacific Ocean and Half Moon Bay, with beach access to both shores. Sitting along the South Jetty, the

Photo by Emily Rieman

Photo by Emily Rieman

Surf dog Nelson hangs out in the camper van while his peeps' suits dry.

park is a popular destination for surfing and fishing. When the surf's up, the Westhaven parking lot is packed full of cars with surfboards strapped to the roof and all shapes and sizes of dogs walking and running about with their people. Before, after or in-between surf sessions your dog can run free and play on the long expanse of beach. Whether you surf or not, Westhaven State Park is a fun and friendly place to hang out, much like Westport itself.

If you don't have your own equipment for enjoying the surf, you can rent boards and wetsuits at the **Surf Shop**. The Surf Shop has been around for at least 20 years and can advise novices and experts on all things surf related in Westport. The friendly staff will connect you with experienced, local surfers for lessons or you can check out a surf camp. Once you have your gear, whether you choose to take a lesson or just wing it on your own, Westhaven State Park is perfect for beginner's pop-up practice in the white water and more challenging waves for the more advanced if you paddle out to the line up. For beginners, the waves are friendlier in the summer and fall months.

With 18 miles of beautiful, sandy beach, groomed trails, awesome waves and dog-friendly accommodations, Westport is the perfect Fido-friendly surf getaway. 🐾

MORE INFORMATION

Vacations by the Sea
260 East Dock Street, Westport
360.268.1119; vacationbythesea.com

Glenacres Historic Inn
222 Montesano Street, Westport
360.268.0958; glenacresinn.com

Westport Marina Cottages
481 E. Neddie Rose Drive, Westport
360.268.1119; marinacottages.com

Islander Motel
421 Neddie Rose Drive, Westport
360.268.7682; islanderwestport.com

The Mermaid Deli
200 East Patterson, Westport
360.612.0435; mermaiddeli.com

The Surf Shop
4207 N Montesano Street, Westport
360.268.0992; westportsurfshop.com

Photo by Emily Rieman

Copalis Beach

CLAM DIGGING AND BEACH COMBING, COMPLETE WITH A CANINE-FRIENDLY RESORT.

The Washington coast is calling and Iron Springs Resort has your number. There are miles of beache to explore, rainforests to wander, waves to watch crash on the shore With the cozy, dog-friendly cabins of **Iron Springs Resort** you can head out for a retreat with your four-legged friend by your side. These are the special ingredients that make Iron Springs the perfect treat for you and your pooch.

STAY Located along Washington's North Beach coastline, the property sits perched above the Pacific Ocean. It's a secluded place, with just 25 cabins on 20 acres, flanked by forest on one side and water on the other. Also on property is a General Store, guest laundry and a clam station. That is it, and it is all you and Fido will need.

About a three hour drive from Seattle, you and your dog will be greeted by the resort's staff who play with your pup, and help you check in and purchase any provisions you may want at the General Store. Open daily until 7 p.m., it's small, but packed with most everything you might need for your stay including a wide range of food, beverages—including wine, and assorted sundries. It is worth noting, that a visit to Iron Springs cannot go without baking a batch

Photos by Julie Clegg

Clockwise from top: Guests at Iron Springs have easy access to the beach; Sheeba greets four-legged guests to the resort; cabins sit perched on a bluff overlooking the beach; the general store is stocked for pups; everything you need for the beach.

GETTING HERE From Seattle, follow I-5 S. At Olympia, use right two lanes to take exit 104 for US-101. Follow US-101 for about five miles then WA-8 W for 20 miles. At Aberdeen, follow signs to Ocean Shores then WA-109 N for approximately 30 miles.

bove: Scout enjoys a rest back at the cabin after a long day at
he beach. Right: Iron Springs provides towels for its furry guests.

f amazingly delicious cinnamon rolls. Pick up a packet of this mix for
aking later, and enjoy the deliciousness made famous by the resort's
ounder Olive Little. In 1947, Olive Little bought Iron Springs Resort and
t the time, it was just eight cabins and a main lodge. Soon after, Ms. Little
xpanded the lodge and opened a restaurant, where she turned out her fa-
nous clam chowder and cinnamon rolls. As the resort grew more popular,
he continued to add cabins, carefully considering placement and orienta-
on to take advantage of the breathtaking views and amazing location.

As with any property of this age, Iron Springs was in need of a facelift
nd in the Summer of 2010, restoration began. The new owners wanted
o keep the resort's charm and integrity while adding some much-needed
pdates. When you explore the property and your cabin, you will see that
hey definitely accomplished their goal.

While the cabins are charming and cozy, modern upgrades include com-
letely renovated kitchens with dishwashers, modernized and enlarged
athroom, new furniture throughout, restored fireplaces or wood burning
toves, new wood floors, flat-screen satellite TV with DVD player for the
ong list of movies you can borrow at the General Store, new windows, bar-
ecues, outdoor water spigots and hoses for washing sand off your pooch,
ew siding, insulation and decks, WiFi throughout the resort, and a new
lam cleaning station located near the beach.

The improvements have not gone unnoticed as one guest notes, "We
irst came to visit Iron Springs in 1987 with our friends who suggested we
ake Cabin 14. We fell in love with it. We've been back every year since."

PLAY Returning guests is a common theme at Iron Springs and you
can see why when you visit. Coastal
activities abound, from kite flying
to beach combing. You can even
arrange for horseback riding on the
beach with **Chenois Creek Horse
Rentals**. They have horses available
for beginners to advanced riders, no
appointment necessary. If you are
looking for some additional relaxation, **Blue Spa** offers 60 or 90 minute
in-cabin massages for Iron Springs
guests. After, take your pup to the
beach and make your way down the
trail to the water for a sight to be-
hold. Miles of sandy beach stretches
out in either direction, waves crash
on the shore, and the Pacific Ocean
stretches endlessly on the horizon.

At low tide, walk out to Copalis
Rock and find little shell keepsakes in
the sand; or explore the Iron Springs
Walking Loop to experience the

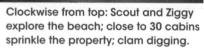

Clockwise from top: Scout and Ziggy explore the beach; close to 30 cabins sprinkle the property; clam digging.

Depending on the time of year, you are also in razor clam country. Clamming is a seasonal sport and a shellfish license is required. For just a nominal amount, you can purchase a three-day razor clam license from the Washington Department of Fish & Wildlife for a weekend of fun. The Pacific razor clam is one of the most sought after shellfish in the state of Washington and Iron Springs has all of the gear, like shovel, clam tube, and mesh bag, that you'll need to dig. There is also a covered, cleaning station on the property, with a nearby fireplace and bench to warm your toes plus a horseshoe pit if you are so inclined. If you are lucky enough to come away from your dig with a bushel of clams, you will find several recipes back at the cabin in the "Everything Book," including Olive Little's infamous clam chowder, fried clams and a recipe for the "best darn razor clam dip ever."

During your stay at Iron Springs, if you need to pick up pet supplies, swing into the **Salty Dog** (*shopsaltydog.com*). Featuring a full range of fun and functional products for playing, eating, sleeping and wearing, the Salty Dog will help you make the most of a trip to the beach, a walk in the woods or an evening by the fire. 🐾

silence of nature. Inland hikes are easy and relatively short, with easy access to the beach. Grab a map at the General Store, along with some treats and water for you and Fido, and head out for some fun. This region of Washington tends to attract birders from all over the country and nearby Hoquiam is home of the nationally recognized Shorebird Festival. Hundreds of thousands of shorebirds migrate from Central and South America to the Arctic each spring, stopping at the nutrient rich mud flats of the Grays Harbor National Wildlife Refuge.

PLAY The region is also home to a number of state and national parks. **Griffiths-Priday Ocean State Park** is a 364-acre marine park with 8,316 feet of saltwater shoreline on the Pacific Ocean and 9,950 feet of freshwater shoreline on the Copalis River. The park extends from the beach through low dunes to the river, then north to the river's mouth. The Copalis Spit Natural Area, a designated wildlife refuge, is also part of the park.

MORE INFORMATION

Iron Springs Resort
3707 Highway 109
Copalis Beach, Wash.
Phone: 360.276.4230
Toll-free: 1.800.380.7950
ironspringsresort.com

Long Beach Peninsula

PACIFIC OCEAN TO THE WEST, COLUMBIA RIVER TO THE SOUTH, AND WILLAPA BAY TO THE EAST.

LONG BEACH Perched on the ocean, in the heart of Long Beach, Washington, is a modern and unique hotel with an emphasis on value, sustainability and of course, dog friendliness. As you pull into the parking lot at the **Adrift Hotel** in Long Beach, Wash., You'll be struck by its proximity to the Pacific Ocean. You can smell the salty air and hear the waves crashing on the shore.

Owners, Brady and Tiffany Turner, acquired the 80-room Adrift Hotel in 2011 with a particular vision in mind. Formerly an outdated economy motel, they wanted to create a hotel that was unique, modern, fun and relaxed—an oceanfront retreat for all types of travelers to fully enjoy, two-and four-legged alike. And, that's exactly what they did.

Clockwise from top: Life is good at Long Beach; some off-leash fun for Thya; grab a beach cruiser provided by the Adrift Hotel and enjoy a ride along the eight-mile Discovery Trail; fields of tall grass line the shore; a happy Ziggy enjoys the beach.

After a complete renovation, the décor is modern, with a minimalist, relaxed vibe to it. The couple also remodeled the hotel with the environment and sustainability in mind. Much of the fixtures and furnishings throughout the property are reclaimed and recycled. Through its operations, the hotel

GETTING HERE From Seattle, take I-5 S, WA-8 W and US-12 W to Montesano. Take the exit toward WA-107/Montesano/Raymond om US-12 W to connect with US-101. Take US-101 S to WA-103 N in Pacific County for approximately 70 miles.

Photos by Julie Clegg

Top: Thya makes herself at home at the Adrift Hotel. **Above, from left:** Enjoy a game of shuffleboard; mason jars with candles light the tables at Pickled Fish; decorative lights above the front desk.

uses green and recycled products as much as possible. And, because the Adrift treats dogs as family, you'll want to bring your pup with you when you check in for a little staff play time before walking to your oceanfront room. The view is incredible and the room comes with a king size bed with a memory foam mattress, table and two chairs, a large flat screen TV, DVD player, music docking station, small fridge and free WiFi. All that's left for you to do is lay out your dog's bed and comfort items, and then grab some water, snacks and Fido and go outside for a little adventure.

The beautiful, 21-mile Long Beach Peninsula consists of six small communities, Ilwaco, Long Beach, Nahcotta, Ocean Park, Oysterville, and Seaview, with each town having its own charm. There are also two lighthouses, plenty of parks, miles and miles of driftwood covered beaches, and the **Discovery Trail**, an amazing eight-mile paved trail through the dunes running parallel to the Pacific. The Discovery Trail is perfect for walking, running and especially biking. Hop on one of the hotel's complimentary beach cruisers and pedal to your heart's content. The trail follows Captain William Clark's first oceanside hike in 1805 from Ilwaco

to Long Beach. Today, the eight-mile stretch features interpretive markers, an authentic whale skeleton, a 20-foot bronze tree and several statues.

If you cruise into town, the main drag is lined with an array of locally-owned, small businesses, from kite shops to ice cream parlors to pizza joints to surf shops and most have a "Pets Welcome" sign hanging in their window. Stop by **Paws By the Sea** in Long Beach for a great selection of doggy supplies. Visit the North Beach Candy Man also in Long Beach and ask for some of their Scottie Dog-shaped red or black licorice candy. This area is brimming with restaurants with pet-friendly patios where you can get all different types of seafood, chowders, pub grub, pizza, and pasta. We recommend The Cove, Blue Collar Eats, Galletti's Spaghetti House, Hungry Harbor Grille, and the Corral Drive-In. It's worth noting that while leash laws are not typically enforced on the beach for well-behaved dogs, there is an eight-foot leash law within city limits.

If you've done all your exploring and want to skip in-town eating, just head back to the Adrift Hotel to the **Pickled Fish**, located on the top floor overlooking the ocean. Like the hotel itself, the ambience is cool, with candles in mason jars to light the tables, a chalkboard wall highlighting the week's live music and a menu that is divine. From crab mac 'n cheese to wood fired pizzas, there is a little something for everyone. We recommend the sautéed wild Alaskan salmon, with a mixed green salad and

per aioli. If a drink is in
rder, check the chalkboard
r the day's cocktail or
hoose from several regional
ines and Northwest
microbrews on the menu.

The Adrift has many
nique touches to appreciate.
addition to the compli-
entary beach cruisers,
ere are also foosball and
huffleboard tables onsite,
ovies, books and games
ou can borrow, and compli-
entary organic coffee, tea
d filtered fruit water in the
bby at all times. Also in the
bby are items for purchase
cluding wine, beer, soda
d snacks, including Spark-
an's Wilderness Red wine,
g Al Rat City Blonde beer,
nteman's Cherry Tree Cola,

Thya finds herself right at home in one of the Sou'wester's vintage trailers.

heo's Organic Salted Almond Milk Chocolate. If you accidently forgot to
ing dog food, they have Portland, Oregon's own Castor + Pollux on hand.

In addition to the Adrift Hotel, the Turners also own the Inn at Discovery
oast, located next door. With a bit more luxury in mind, the rooms at the Inn
ature a jetted tub, fireplace and private balcony. The Inn is also pet friendly
the first floor.

EAVIEW Is "glamping" your thing? Urban Dictionary defines glamping as
Glamorous camping that satisfies your craving for the outdoors, but serves
our penchant for a good meal, nice glass of wine, and a comfortable bed."
ound like something you'd like to check out? Here at CityDog we take our
amping seriously, and after researching the **Glamping With Pets** website — a
te entirely dedicated to glamping with pets — we discovered the **Sou'wester**
Seaview, Wash.

The Sou'wester is more quaint than glamorous, with a hodgepodge of
te, little cabins, vintage travel trailers, a lodge built in 1892, and about 20
mpsites and RV hookups. It will feel like you are stepping back in time to
our childhood. When you stroll into the lodge to check-in, some cool music
ill be emoting from the record player, it's all vinyl at the Sou'wester.
here's not a TV in sight or phones ringing off the hook, no hustle or bustle,
st a laid back groovy vibe that you and your pooch will love.

When you make your reser-
vation let the Sou'wester know
that you want to stay in the
Spartan Mansion. In trailer terms
the Spartan is a mansion with a
kitchen, private bedroom with a
double bed, tiny bathroom, living
room plus two single bunk beds
that serve as a second bedroom.
It's cozy enough for two adults
and two dogs, and the décor is a
mix of 1950s kitsch. There's even
a record player, with a selection
of vinyl picked out by the good
people at Sou'Wester sitting on
the turntable for you to enjoy, or
bring your own.

Once you have your pup's
bedding and water bowl situated,
head out to explore the grounds.
You and Fido must make a stop
at the **Thrifty**, a vintage camper

Photo by Amelia Soper

Photos by Amelia Soper

Clockwise from top: More off-leash fun; bunk beds in the Spartan Mansion; 'kitchy' kitchen in the Spartan; Thrifty, a vintage camper with a tiny thrift store inside.

with a tiny thrift store inside. Everything is on the honor system. After you find a few items you need to purchase, just head back to the lodge to pay for what you owe. Easy and honest. At the lodge, there is also a small general store, with various sundries such as locally-made soaps and essential oils, handcrafted jewelry and artwork plus snacks, sodas, beer and wine. The store is also on the honor system. Once you are ready to pay, write down what you selected on piece of paper, slip the note and your cash in the envelope provided and deposit it through the mail slot.

After you have purchased all of the things you need, head backout and meander past the **Mamook Spa**, located in a renovated 1954 Boles Aero camper. Services include therapeutic massage and bodywork plus guests can participate in meditation, community gatherings, wellness workshops, and more in the adjacent Pavilion. Located nearby is the **Finnish Sauna** and

Garden Spa. The dry sauna is built out of clear western cedar, with hand-milled Port Orford Cedar benches. The garden spa features a gorgeous changing and showering room plus an outdoor clawfoot tub for cooling off. These luxuries will come in handy after a day exploring the area, hiking, trail running, kayaking, or maybe even a little paddleboarding.

For first time visitors we recommend grabbing one of the Sou'wester vintage bikes and heading to the beach. Tip: bring your doggy bicycle carriage to connect it to the back of the bike and have fun pedaling about the relatively flat area, giving your dog a first hand look at things. The beach is only about a block away, and makes for an easy time if your dog is in its bicycle carriage or trotting alongside you as you pedal. Once at the Pacific, you'll see waves crashin

bove: The Sou'wester features a fleet of vintage travel trailers
vailable for nightly rentals. Right: It's all vintage, even the music.

d your dog will be in heaven, frolicking in the surf and racing as
st as their little paws can carry them along the wide open beach that
retches for miles. Leash laws are not typically enforced on the beach,
ovided dogs are controlled and well-behaved. Always remember to
ck up after your pooch's potty plops. 🐾

ORE INFORMATION

rift Hotel
9 Sid Snyder Drive
ong Beach, Wash.
0.561.2456
rifthotel.com

ng Beach Peninsula
sitors Bureau
4 Pacific Way
aview, Wash.
0.451.2542; funbeach.com

Sou'wester Lodge
3728 J Place
Seaview, Wash.
360.642.2542
souwesterlodge.com

Glamping With Pets
pets.glampinghub.com

Photos by Amelia Soper

Seattle & North Puget Sound

In a city that boasts more dogs than children, it's no surprise that Seattle consistently ranks in the top five dog friendliest cities in the country.

Photo by Jamie Pflughoeft

DOWNTOWN
DOG LOUNGE
EST 2002

COME STAY WITH US

Playcare, Overnights, Grooming & Training

Ballard
824 NW 46th St
Seattle, WA 98107

South Lake Union
1011 Mercer St
Seattle, WA 98109

New clients please register online at:
bit.ly/DDLdogs

206.309.8793

SEATTLE IS CALLED THE EMERALD CITY FOR A GOOD REASON: ITS LOCATION. SURROUNDED BY WATER WITH THE PUGET SOUND TO THE WEST, LAKE WASHINGTON TO THE EAST, AND NESTLED IN MOUNTAINS AND EVERGREEN FORESTS, THE CITY IS HOME TO THOUSANDS OF ACRES OF PARKLAND FOR YOU TO ENJOY.

ow considered a high-tech town, Seattle's roots are grounded in iendly, industrious, artistic, music-loving people who are fanatical out their dogs. As the saying goes, Seattle is home to more dogs an it is to children! Even Seattle's businesses can't get enough dog ne. Online retail giant Amazon has its dog-digging headquarters Seattle, and welcomes over 2,000 pups on their campus every day here they enjoy dog-level drinking fountains, complimentary treats, d a 1,000 square-foot dog park. If you are an absolute dog fanatic en Seattle is the town for you.

With over 14 dog parks, numerous in-city recreational areas, and g-friendly places to stay and eat, Seattle has all it takes for you and ur pup to enjoy a great getaway. Also transportation really isn't an sue as Seattle's Metro Transit buses and the Seattle Center Monorail adly transport leashed dogs and their humans. There's also a high umber of dog-accepting Uber drivers in this pooch-centric city, and ts in carriers can join you when you rent a car through car2go. en the Washington State Ferry system allows dogs, which comes

in handy if you visit a nearby island. All of these options come in handy as you travel about Seattle, making time to stop and toss fish at Pike Place Market, listen to some music at the Museum of Pop Culture, and walk the grounds of the Chihuly Garden and Glass located next to the Space Needle.

There are so many dog-friendly things to do in Seattle you may feel overwhelmed. Never fear, as we tried nearly all of them in order to provide you with our top picks. From hotels that pamper your pooch, to restaurants that welcome you and Fido through the front door, and everything else in-between, here are our selections for things to do while in the Seattle area with your dog.

Photos by Julie Clegg

Seattle

THE EMERALD CITY BECKONS WITH A PLETHORA OF DOG-FRIENDLY PLACES TO PLAY.

Seattle is a city made up of distinct neighborhoods, home to coffee, grunge music, museums, high tech companies, farmers markets, gastronomic delights and a diverse population that welcome dog lovers. Over 120 districts and neighborhoods combine to create the culture of Seattle, and no two are alike. From the Norwegian-infused burrough of Ballard to the beachy vibe of Alki Beach on the westside of town, Seattle has a lot for you to enjoy. Here are our must-see things to do in and around Seattle with your pup.

WEST SEATTLE West Seattle could be called a neighborhood of neighbor-hoods. A quick search online lists 24 neighborhoods within West Seattle alone. From Alki on the north end to White Center on the south end, West Seattle is a dog lover's dream.

On a sunny day in Seattle, the hot spot is Alki, a long strip of beach that extends from Alki Point to the Du-wamish Head on Elliott Bay. It's the perfect place for a stroll any time of year, but especially in the spring and summer, it draws joggers, roller blad-ers, volleyball players, beachcombers, sunbathers, bicyclists and of course, dog lovers. If you're lucky and it's a sunny day, grab an outdoor table on the spa-cious deck at **Slices** and order a bucket of beer and pizza by the slice, while taking in the plethora of people and pooches walking by on "The Ave."

For a little pick-me-up post pizza, hop over to **Pioneer Coffee**, located ght next door. The interior tiny, but the outside seating area is spacious. Grab latte and mingle for a bit before meandering north n Alki Avenue for a stop the Statue of Liberty, a ift from the Boy Scouts f America in 1952 and a opular West Seattle gathering place.

Unfortunately, the sandy each area at Alki is off mits to dogs, but the main ath that runs 2.5 miles long the water is perfect or dog walking.

Take the short jaunt up to dmiral Way and California venue for a stop at **Mud ay**. Mud Bay is a locally wned business, with 20+ et stores throughout the uget Sound area. In addition to more han 500 formulas of cat and dog food, Mud Bay carries a wide assortment of reats, toys and accessories as well as eatures local artists and photographers.

Further south on California Avenue, s one of West Seattle's most bustling neighborhoods, the Alaska Junction— r "the Junction" as locals call it. Here, ou will find the infamous Easy Street Records, clothing boutiques, used bookstores and most notably, **Next to Nature**. This locally- and independently-owned pet store has been around since 1995, offering only the healthiest, ll-natural foods and treats for your bets as well as a wide array of toys, collars, leashes and other accessories for discerning dogs.

Located nearby, is **Hotwire Online Coffeehouse**—part coffee bar, part Internet café. Grab a cappuccino with

Photo by Julie Clegg

Previous page, clockwise from top: Skateboarding is a favorite pasttime along Alki; Hotwire Online Coffee House is Fido friendly; order a bucket of beer with your pizza at Slices; Gus perched on a piece of driftwood at Lincoln Park; Gus and Ransom wait in line for a latte at Pioneer Coffee. Above: Lincoln Park.

your canine, and enjoy free wireless on your laptop or hop on one of their computers—the purchase of a tasty beverage grants you 15 minutes of Internet access on their machines.

Next, head south on California Avenue to Fauntleroy Way, turn right and follow it to **Lincoln Park**. One of Seattle's best parks, Lincoln includes 4.6 miles of walking paths, 3.9 miles of bike trails, five picnic shelters, acres of playfields, and an outdoor heated saltwater pool and bathhouse. Dogs aren't allowed in the pool, but there are plenty of places to explore including a forested area at the top with miles of trails and a mile long walkway along the waterfront.

As the day closes, head back on Fauntleroy Way to the Morgan Junction. The Morgan Junction is not as bustling as the Alaska Junction, with as many shops and restaurants, but it is home to one place not to be missed, the **Beveridge Place Pub**. The Beveridge is a dog friendly oasis, with 25 beers on draught and over 100 bottled selections as well as wine, sparklers and ciders.

Also located in the Morgan Junction is the **Wash Dog**, a do-it-yourself or they-can-do-it-for-you bathhouse and spa for your dog, complete with all the ingredients to make your pooch sparkle. Further south on California Avenue is **Good Dog** daycare, boarding and grooming and be sure to swing by **Pet Elements** for high quality food and treats plus toys and other pet accessories.

Photo by Julie Clegg

Nelson and Brad are geared up for skateboarding along Alki.

Worth a mention is White Center, located on the very south end of West Seattle. White Center, and adjacent Westwood, have evolved into a funky, family- and dog-friendly neighborhood. Thirsty? Swing by the **Triangle Tavern**, where dogs are welcome. In need of some food and treats? Head to **A Dog's Dream** or **Pet Pros**. Also located near White Center, is **Westcrest Off Leash Area**. Westcrest is a mixture of developed park and second growth forest covering 80-plus acres, with plenty of on-leash trails plus an off-leash area featuring a large fenced play area plus a small dog/shy dog play area.

MORE INFORMATION

Slices
2600 Marine Ave SW, Seattle
206.935.0178; slicesonalki.com

Mud Bay
2611 California Ave SW, Seattle
206.932.0911; Mudbay.us

Pioneer Coffee
2536 Alki Ave SW, Seattle
206.937.0920

Hotwire Coffeehouse
4410 California Ave SW, Seattle
206.935.1510; hotwirecoffee.com

Pet Elements
6701 California Ave SW, Seattle
206.932.0457; petelements.com

Next to Nature
4543 California Ave SW, Seattle
206.935.1134; next-to-nature.com

Beveridge Place Pub
6413 California Ave SW, Seattle
beveridgeplacepub.com

Wash Dog
6400 California Ave SW, Seattle
206.935.4546; thewashdog.com

Good Dog Daycare
7003 California Ave SW, Seattle
206.932.7833; gooddog-inc.com

Westcrest Off Leash Area
9000 8th Ave SW, Seattle
seattle.gov/parks

PIONEER SQUARE Another part of Seattle that will welcome you with open arms is the Pioneer Square neighborhood. Pioneer Square lays claim to many things, the birthplace of Seattle and now for its canine-friendliness! Pioneer Square is Seattle' original downtown neighborhood, ric in people and pet history. The mix of old Seattle architecture, contemporary shops, and an abundance of good eats and activities make it a must-see for locals and visitors alike, and doggie day trippers.

Long been a place for visitors, settlers arrived in the area in 1852, and Pioneer Square truly hit its stride after being rebuilt following Seattle's Great Fire of 1889 that destroyed the entire core business district of Seattle. Rather than rebuilding in the marshy tide flats left behind, the city decided to fill the area and build brick and stone buildings atop the charred remains. Many o the buildings you now see in this area sit at least 20 feet above the original street level.

Before you go out and explore the rich history of the area, you'll want to square away your hotel. There are not many hotels in the Pioneer Square neighborhood, but that is immaterial as we've found one in an excellent location within steps to Pioneer Square. The **Alexis Hotel** welcomes all guests with a warm smile and a kind word, and guests with dogs will enjoy a welcome that includes signage that greets their canine by name! The Alexis treats dogs just like they treat their human guests, where visiting pooches are provided with treats and dog beds that match the Alexis' signature guest bath robes. Pooch pampering is why celebrities, such as pop music star Rihanna, choose the Alexis. Also the décor gives a sense

Photos by Tushna Lehman

f Seattle without ever
aving the hotel, including
rt collections that spotlight
Northwest artists and iconic
eattle art entities. The bou-
que Alexis Hotel will ar-
ange for in-room dog sitting
hile you explore the city
nd enjoy the gastronomic
elights served in the hotel's
estaurant, the Library Bistro
nd Bookstore Bar.

After spending time
ith Fido and getting him
alked, and acclimated
o the hotel it's time to go
xplore the Pioneer Square
eighborhood. Start with
ne of the most interesting
ours Seattle offers. After the
ig fire, the city condemned
nuch of the area, left bare
nd underground from
he fire for fear of bubonic
lague. The underground
rea became home to illegal
ophouses, gambling halls,
peakeasies, and other
ssorted activities. The **Bill
peidel's Underground
our** provides a glimpse into
his original area, entombed
torefronts and sidewalks
ia walking through the
ubterranean passages when
he city was rebuilt on top of
self after the Great Fire. The color-
ul, all-ages appropriate commen-
ary not only educates, it entertains
n the 75-minute tour.

After the tour, take a stroll in
Pioneer Place Park and enjoy some
hade under the Iron Pergola built in
909. Built the same year, the nearby
ronze bust of Chief Seattle honors
he Native-American leader's local

Top: Relaxing with a book at Zeitgeist Coffee. Above: Waterfall Garden Park.

legacy. For canine history buffs, it also originally marked a water fountain
used by dogs and horses.

During the Klondike Gold Rush of the 1890s, the Pioneer Square area
became a bustling business district, and newspapers wrote about the
prospectors and their "teams of trained dogs, trotting about" town. At the
Klondike Gold Rush National Historic Park/Visitor Center, learn about
the era, pan for gold or join one of the ranger-led walking tours of Pioneer
Square. Tours end at the Smith Tower, built in 1914, when it was one of
the world's first skyscrapers. Ride the original brass and copper elevator to
visit the 35th-floor, an open-air observation deck where you have a 360 de-

Photos by Tushna Lehman

Clockwise from top: The Alexis Hotel welcomes dogs; enjoy a sandwich at Salumi; Harrison hangs out at Globe Book Store.

gree view of Seattle. When done taking in the sites, step inside for a cocktail in the Tower's speakeasy themed bar.

Once back at ground level, make your way to the **Seattle Metropolitan Police Museum** and **Last Resort Fire Department Museum** that depicts life in uniform from the 1800s to present. For law enforcement enthusiasts, the Police Museum showcases weaponry, artifacts and even a historic jail cell. Opened in 2008, the Fire Museum showcases historical vehicles, such as an 1834 hand-pumper, older than Washington State itself. In addition to learning about Seattle's Great Fire, ask about Smokey, the fire house's former, resident Dalmatian.

Now that you've gotten your history fix, it's time to collect Fido and head out to find a meal for you and a snack for your pup. To satisfy your puppy's palate, head to the **Rocky Mountain Chocolate Factory**, which offers "chocolate-dipped" dog bones packaged in paw-print cellophane

bags. Not true chocolate, they bones are scrumptious and safe for canine consumption. For the human sweet tooth, cases are filled with truffles, locally-made ice cream, giant caramel apples and everything from chocolate-dipped Oreos to Twinkies. Dog lovers will especially love Rocky Mountain's "Bark" candy in various flavors.

Pioneer Square is filled with some of Seattle's delectable and famous places to grab a meal. **Salumi Artisan Cured Meats** is world-renowned for artisanal Italian cured meats that will have you salivating. Opened in 1999 by Armandino Batali, Salumi serves sandwiches, soups, and pastas, created from recipes based on Italian tradition and refreshed with innovation, to a hungry lunchtime crowd. Lines snake around the block at Salumi's where your canine companion can help ease the wait, and maybe even sneak a few free meat samples!

While you may be one of the lucky few to find a seat inside Salumi's, since you have your dog in-tow head on over to the **Waterfall Garden Park**. This hidden gem has plenty of outdoor seating surrounded by azaleas, rhododendrons and geraniums. The 22-foot waterfall makes it an oasis for everyone, including Fido, to enjoy. Or, walk to **Occidental Park** in the heart of the historic Pioneer Square, where trees provide plenty of shade and outdoor furniture, and

earby outdoor café areas
rovide places to relax. Oc-
dental Park has bocce ball
urts and ping pong tables
r you to participate or just
atch the friendly competi-
on; and there are bookstores,
rt galleries, boutiques, and
ther unique shops for you
nd your pup to enjoy.

Pioneer Pet Feed and
upply is Pioneer Square's
oggie hotspot. Another
nderground area gem,
wner David Bovard opened
e shop in 2012, partially to
onor his dog Irko. A tattoo
n Bovard's bicep memorial-
es the precious pup. The
hop exudes old-world charm
anks to original, rounded
oorways, stained-glass lamps
nd antique, pet-themed
ostcards decorating the
ounter. The store stocks a
ariety of local, Northwest
roducts and is dedicated to
ealthy, affordable options.
our dog will go wild for the
Singles Snack Bar," an old-
shioned, apothecary-style
og deli where glass jars filled
ith tasty treats such as sweet
otato slices, freeze-dried
heddar cheese bits and hemp
anana treats, tempt your dog
ith glorious smells.

If you are looking for a
ovel experience, drop by the
lobe Bookstore. An antique
dition of Rin Tin Tin graces
he display window hinting
t the store's doggie devotion.
wner John Siscoe invites
ibliophiles and their dogs to
xplore the stacks of books
lanketing every wall.

Kicking back at Shotgun Ceremonies.

Photo by Julie Clegg

MORE INFORMATION

Alexis Hotel
1007 1st Ave, Seattle
206.624-.4844; alexishotel.com

Bill Speidel's Underground Tour
608 First Avenue
206.682.4646; undergroundtour.com

Klondike Gold Rush Visitor Center
319 Second Avenue
206.220.4240; nps.gov/klse

Smith Tower
506 Second Avenue South
206.622.4004; smithtower.com

Seattle Metropolitan Police Museum
317 Third Avenue South; 206.748.9991
seametropolicemuseum.org

Cherry Street Coffee House
103 Cherry Street
206.621.9372; cherryst.com

Zeitgeist Coffee
171 South Jackson Street
206.583.0497; zeitgeistcoffee.com

Salumi Artisan Cured Meats
309 Third Avenue South
206.621.8772; salumicuredmeats.com

Waterfall Garden Park
NW corner of 2nd Ave S and S Main St

The Central Saloon
207 First Avenue South
206.622.0209; centralsaloon.com

Pioneer Pet Feed & Supply
87 1/2 South Washington Street
206.437.8566; pioneerpetseattle.com

Globe Bookstore
218 First Avenue South; 206.682.6882

Sam Day Studio & Gallery
79 South Main Street
206.382.7413; samday.com

Penny's Old Time Portrait Studio
112 South Washington Street
206.467.1547; klondikepennys.com

Shotgun Ceremonies
206 First Avenue South
206.372.3349; shotgunceremonies.com

Rocky Mountain Chocolate Factory
99 Yesler Way; 206.405.2872
rockymountainchocolatefactory.com

Last Resort Fire Department Museum
301 Second Avenue South
206.783.4474; lastresortfd.org

Photos by Amelia Soper

Clockwise from top: Point Robinson Beach and Lighthouse; Nashi Orchards; relax at Vashon Lodges; the Lodges' outdoor patio.

VASHON ISLAND In Seattle's backyard is the lively and artistic community of Vashon Island. This little gem has beautiful beaches, truly wonderful places to stay that will welcome you and your pup, eclectic restaurants, and quaint shops that, when added up together, create an artistic getaway that you will cherish for years to come. Just a short ferry ride from Seattle, hop on one of the big boats, for a short ride across the water, and you'll be dropped off into a little piece of paradise.

Start by checking into the lovely and dog friendly **Lodges on Vashon**. If a pet parent were to design the perfect setting for communal living, the Lodge would be it. First, they feature two common spaces, the Public House and the Pavilion. The Public House features complimentary coffee and tea, an ice maker and lounge room, where you can eat dinner with friends and fellow lodgers at the large table or steal away to a corner and catch up on email. The Pavilion features an open-air patio, with firepit, heat lamps, cozy seating areas and a comfy couch for relaxing by the gigantic gas fireplace with Fido.

Located along the tree-lined edge of the property are the Meadow Lodges that feature a separate bedroom with king size bed, seating area with gas fireplace, a well-stocked wet bar, and a cozy nook with a trundle bed for two. Best of all, the bathroom features French doors that open onto a private outdoor patio where you can take in the fresh air while you shower; and there's ample room for two, plus in-floor radiant heat, handmade soaps and amenities from local artisans and super soft terry cloth towels. When you are walking the grounds make sure to keep your pup on a leash as there are plenty of deer that roam the grounds.

Photos by Amelia Soper

From left: Enjoy a scoop at Glass Bottle Creamery; Vashon Lodges.

After you've settled in and taken [ca]re of your gear and your pup's [ne]eds, take an easy stroll to down[to]wn Vashon, where you won't be [ab]le to resist stopping at the **Glass [B]ottle Creamery** for homemade ice [cr]eam. Dogs enjoy a scoop of plain [va]nilla, while the humans tend to [go] a bit more exotic with a straw[be]rry balsamic swirl or chocolate [ch]ip with fresh mint.

When you feel like moving on, [yo]ur next visit should be **Nashi [O]rchards**, where they make small [ba]tch, hard cider to taste and take [h]ome. Upon arrival you are most [li]kely to be greeted by the resident [Bo]uviers who help lend some [fri]endliness and humor to the [or]chards. While the dogs frolic in [th]e adjacent orchard, take a sip of [be]rry, pear cider; or our favorite, [th]e award winning Chojuro, made [w]ith Asian pears. Chojuro is super [cr]isp, not too sweet and it'll be hard [to] resist buying some to take back to [th]e Lodges to enjoy in the evening.

After dropping the pup at your home-away-from-home for the night, the Lodges, head back into the core area of town for a meal at **May Restaurant and Bar**. While May is the only Thai restaurant on Vashon, it is one of the best in all of Seattle. Start with an appetizer of fried watercress and slowly make your way to finish with their famous Phad Thai, perfectly paired with a glass of Dragon's Head Cider, which is also made locally.

Return to the Lodges for a nice evening where you can look up in the sky and see the stars, and hear the summer locust as they skim along the night breezes. Your pup will enjoy a walk around the Lodge's area, sniffing all of the country scents that linger in the air. Make sure to sit a while, taking in the coolness of the evening, snuggling up by the gas fireplace and chatting with your neighbors who have also fallen in love with this retreat on the island. A good night's rest is an easy thing to get when you visit the Lodges. A little artistic, a lot romantic, and perfect for stretching out, staring up into the midnight sky, and dreaming about the adventures left to take with your dog.

Waking in the morning, all ready for a big day playing on the beach, first things first and that means grabbing a latte at **Vashon Island Coffee Roasterie** before heading to **Point Robinson Beach and Lighthouse**, where on a clear, sunny day you can enjoy the view of Mt. Rainier in all its glory. Visiting this part of the island will have you exploring the beach, coming for seashells and driftwood, and listening to the sea life that frolic in the nearby waters. Make sure you keep a keen eye on your pup, picking up as needed, and always provide fresh water, as salt water is not ideal for dogs. You can roam for a long time out on the beach, and if paddleboarding or kayaking is your thing, be sure to pack them so you can enjoy some fun times at Point Robinson.

Photo by Amelia Soper

When you are ready to eat, there are a couple of wonderful delights that we highly recommend. You'll want to try the dog-friendly patio at **The Hardware Store**, famous for its weekend brunch where you can get signature omelets, eggs benedict, french toast, buttermilk pancakes, and bottomless mimosas. If you feel more like a taste of something spicy, then head to **Zamorana** for authentic and delicious Mexican food, where the fish tacos are the best thing you'll have eaten in a long time, and they also have dog-friendly seating outside.

Even if your visit to Vashon Island is short, squeeze in a few more recommendations: Grab a ginger brew or one of the many vegan offerings at **Pure**. Check out the Vashon Island Saturday Farmers Market, open April to December, where you will find all sorts of locally made goods, from soaps to cider. Swing by the pooch-friendly tasting room at **Palouse Winery** or grab a mouthwatering pastry at **Snapdragon** where the back patio is dog-friendly. Definitely make time for **Vashon Island Baking Company**, where the maple donut is to die for! For truly devoted animal lovers, Vashon is home to the **Northwest School of Animal Massage**, offering full, professional certification programs that allow one to become an animal massage therapist. Vashon is also home to the annual **Sheepdog Classic**, which is the most attended herding event on the West Coast. Enjoy local fare, artisan crafts while witnessing working dogs in action.

MORE INFORMATION

Vashon Lodges
17205 Vashon Hwy SW, Vashon
206.693.3750; lodgesonvashon.com

Nashi Orchards
25407 Wax Orchard Rd SW; nashiorchards.com

May Kitchen & Bar
17614 Vashon Hwy SW; maykitchen.com

Vashon Island Coffee Roasterie
19529 Vashon Hwy SW; tvicr.com

Zamorana
17722 Vashon Hwy SW; 206.356.5684

Glass Bottle Creamery
17637 Vashon Hwy SW; 206.463.1033

Palouse Winery
12431 Vashon Hwy SW; palousewinery.com

Point Robinson Beach and Lighthouse
3705 SW Point Robinson Road

Northwest School of Animal Massage
9704 SW 156th Street; nwsam.com

Voted Best Pet Boutique by Seattle A-List!

B.I. BARKERY

EST. 2012

DOG MERCANTILE & BAKED TREATS

A SHOP FOR DOGS AND THE PEOPLE WHO LOVE THEM!

278 Winslow Way E | Located on Beautiful Bainbridge Island
BIBarkery.com | facebook.com/BIBarkery

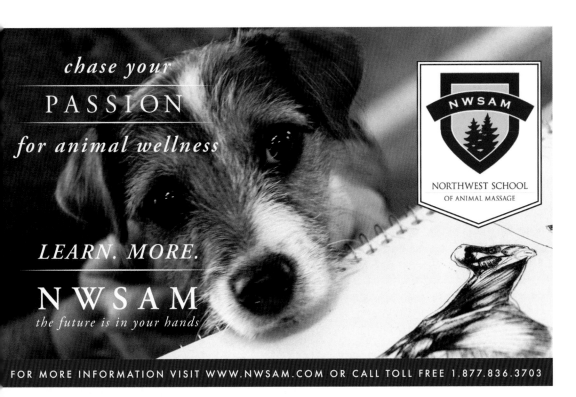

chase your
PASSION
for animal wellness

LEARN. MORE.

N W S A M
the future is in your hands

NWSAM

NORTHWEST SCHOOL
OF ANIMAL MASSAGE

FOR MORE INFORMATION VISIT WWW.NWSAM.COM OR CALL TOLL FREE 1.877.836.3703

Photos by Jen Flynn

Bainbridge Island boasts several beautiful parks including Fay Bainbridge State Park, Eagledale Park and Waterfront Park.

BAINBRIDGE ISLAND Just a 30-minute ferry ride from Seattle, sits beautiful **Bainbridge Island**. Discovered in 1792 by Captain George Vancouver (but settled in the mid-1800's), the Island was later named for naval war hero, Captain William Bainbridge. Today, Bainbridge proudly retains its maritime heritage, just as it has gained a reputation for its beautiful parks.

Bainbridge residents take great care to safeguard their green spaces; no less than 16 parks offer up excellent views and grassy areas (not all are dog-friendly, so check before traveling). For some beach time, make the short drive from the ferry dock to **Fay Bainbridge State Park**, on the northeast corner of the Island. Camping is permitted year-round in this 17-acre park. Pitch a tent with your pup in the shelter of the trees then enjoy the spectacular view of Seattle in one of the Adirondack chairs that are thoughtfully anchored here and there within the reeds. Other parks that are great for leashed walks with your dog: Grand

Forest, Battlepoint Park, Pritchard Park and Gazzam Lake.

Next, head a couple of miles south to **Bainbridge Island Vineyards & Winery** Gerard and Jo Ann Bentryn are the owners of this small family farm, and were the first in the state to produce wines officially declared as "salmon safe," which refers to the purity of their growing and harvesting practices. The grounds, though compact, are nicely landscaped and perfect for a stroll with your pooch before heading into the tasting room to sample some wine.

For off-leash fun, **Eagledale Park** is located on Rose Avenue, south of downtown Winslow and features a quaint little park with a picnic shelter, tennis courts, and an off-leash park.

There is another off-leash park located at **Strawberry Hill Park**, adjacent to a playground and skateboard park. Centrally-located on Bainbridge Island less than three miles from the Bainbridge Ferry Terminal, the wooded, 2.35 acre park features a dog washing station with a hose and spray wand to clean pets before leaving the park. There is also a mini-dog park area for small, shy or recuperating dogs. Inside the park, visitors will find park benches a perimeter walking trail, auto-fill water bowls, and free dog waste collection bags and receptacles.

For post dog park clean up, **Salty Dog Wash and Grooming** is a clean and friendly, state-of-the-art facility, providing a variety of services including a self-serve, do-it-yourself dog wash station (walk-ins okay, supplies provided and best of all, no messy clean up). Or, book an appointment with one of their professional, full service groomers.

Next, grab a bite at Bainbridge's favorite sandwich shop **Fork and Spoon**.

et it to go to enjoy at nearby, 5.5 re **Waterfront Park**, which sits the water just behind the main eet. A location for frequent festivals and other community gatherings, this park is the perfect place to joy sweeping views of the city.

After lunch, explore the shops d boutiques along Winslow Way, any of which are dog friendly. Be re to stop in at **Eagle Harbor Book** . where friendly staff with treats eet you the moment you walk in e door.

Another must-stop is **B.I. Bark-y**, where you will find an abundance of locally sourced, organic eats, food, gear and toys. There's enty of stuff for people too, from g-themed home décor to unique fts for dog lovers.

After shopping, it's time for a ld one at **Bainbridge Brewing**, an dependent craft brewery featuring o locations: **Brewery & Taproom** cated at Coppertop Park (all ages elcome), and **Bainbridge Brewing ehouse** in Downtown Winslow ges 21 and over). There's a lot at goes into making the island's ost delicious brews. The Brewery Taproom and the Bainbridge ewing Alehouse both serve up ore than just deliciously cold pints craft beer. They also have several sty snacks, hard ciders, and soft inks. And at the Alehouse, they er a selection of wines produced island vintners as well as other orthwest and West Coast wines. nce back on the ferry, admire the wntown Seattle skyline glitter-g on the water in the late evening ght, and discuss all the places

It's a lovely day for a stroll among the sailboats at Eagle Harbor.

you'll go the next time you visit Bainbridge Island with Bowzer. It's nice to know that relaxation awaits in such an artistic and welcoming community, just across the water from the hustle and bustle of Seattle.

MORE INFORMATION

Bainbridge Island Vineyards
8989 Day Road East; 206.842.9463
bainbridgevineyards.com

B.I. Barkery
278 Winslow Way East
206.780.8039; bibarkery.com

Eagle Harbor Book Co.
157 Winslow Way East
206.842.5332; eagleharborbooks.com

Fork & Spoon
120 Madrone Lane, North
206.842.3675

Salty Dog Wash & Grooming
4664 Lynwood Center Rd. NE
Suite 129
206.451.4040; saltydogwashbi.com

Brewery & Taproom
9415 Coppertop Loop
bainbridgebeer.com; 206.451.4646

Bainbridge Brewing Alehouse
500 Winslow Way East
bainbridgebeer.com; 206.317.6986

Eagledale Park Off-leash Area
5055 Rose Avenue NE

Strawberry Hill Off-leash Area
7666 High School Rd NE

Fay Bainbridge State Park
15446 Sunrise Dr NE

Waterfront Park
301 Shannon Dr SE

Photo by Jen Flynn

**PICKLES
PLAYLAND**

SMALL-DOG DAYCARE &
ALL-DOG BEER & WINE LOUNGE

Whether you need small-dog daycare or just want to enjoy a beer with your dog while watching the game - Pickles Playland has you covered.

Pickles Playland offers a home-like environment, so you and your dog are always comfortable. Our number one priority is keeping your dog safe.

What we have to offer:

- Small-Dog Daycare (Weekdays)
- Beer & Wine Lounge
  (All Dog-Sizes on Weekends)
- Party Rentals
- Doga Yoga (Every other Saturday)
- Special Events (Movie Night, Classes and More...)

Open Monday-Friday 6am-7pm, Saturday & Sunday 12pm-7pm

12669 NE 85th Street, Kirkland, WA 98033 | 425-298-4530
info@picklesplayland.dog | www.picklesplayland.dog

ASTSIDE The eastside can
e done in a day, a week-
nd, or as long as you have
me to explore; and, its
iversity will keep you and
our pup satisfied no matter
hat things you delve into.
rom skyscrapers that reach
o the sky, beach shores
at ramble along, to nature
kes and waterfalls, the
astside beckons to visitors
om all walks, including the
our-legged type, of life.

Getting to the eastside is
s easy as crossing a bridge.
iterally, as that is what will
et you across Lake Wash-
gton and into the hustle
nd bustle of Bellevue, Red-
ond, Kirkland, Issaquah,
nd even Snoqualmie Falls.
ll of these towns are on the
astside and an easy drive
om one another. Deciding
n where you want to spend
e majority of your time
 key, as there are dog-
iendly hotels throughout
e area.

Love shopping? **Bellevue**
 a shopoholic's dream. Feel
ke an upscale trip to the
hores of Lake Washington,
en **Kirkland** may suit your
astes. Want to enjoy tall
rees and roaring water? You'll absolutely love
verything that **Snoqualmie Falls** has to offer.
o matter where you stop on the eastside, one
lace you must see is the Microsoft Visitor
enter in **Redmond**. While not dog-friendly,
he Center is a must see as it takes you on an
xploration of the history of Microsoft, and
rtificial intelligence, mixed reality, virtual life,
nd video game exhibits. Tip: A quick 10-min-
te drive to **Marymoor Off-Leash Dog Park**,

Photos by Tushna Lehman

From top: With dogs in tow, stroll past the luxury shops at the Bravern; one of the features of a deluxe room at Hotel Bellevue, is the private garden patio.

where you can get your dog tuckered out before heading to the
Microsoft Visitors Center. Marymoor is doggy Disneyland with
40 acres of off-leash area guaranteed to thrill your dog.

BELLEVUE Washington's fifth largest city, Bellevue is first on
our tour, offering the ultimate in retail therapy, dining, and cultural attractions, and yet remains surrounded by natural beauty
and outdoor space. For a place for you and Fido to rest your
head, we highly recommend the **Bellevue Club Hotel**, one of
the city's finest luxury hotels, for your stay in this hip, happening town. With just 66 rooms, it's more boutique than hotel and

Photos by Tushna Lehman

Clockwise from top: Charlie enjoys a stroll at Bellevue Dowtown Park; ready for happy hour at 520 Bar and Grill; the waterfall at Hotel Bellevue; find locally-made products at the Farmers Market.

the service reflects that, with no detail overlooked, for dogs, up to 30-pounds, and humans alike. The dog-friendly deluxe rooms are richly furnished, comple with doggy bed, treats, bottled water, and food and water bowls for your four legged friend.

The king size bed beckons with cushy pillows and soft linens, and the luxurious marble, limestone and granite bathroom has geranium-mint bath salts if a soak in the tub is in orde Guests of the hotel are afforded a hospitality membership to the Club durin their stay, with access to the hotel's full-service spa, indoor and outdoor swimming pools, workout studios, tennis courts, and four restaurants. The Polaris, Cosmos, Splash, and Luna Express restaurants offer everything from a simple morning espresso to lig lunch, to an expertly-made cocktail to dinner inspired by local growers' freshest seasonal ingredients. There is also a cozy library, where you and your pooch are welcome to relax with a cup of tea by the fire All-in-all, a sta at the Bellevue Club Hotel is an urban retreated right in the heart of a big city

After resting up and taking care of things at the hotel, it's time for a little retail indulgence. Located about a mile from Hotel Bellevue, the **Bravern**, is comprised of 309,000 square feet of luxury retail space, a state-of-the-art gym, two office towers, and two residential apartment towers. It is a vibrant and dog-friendly outdoor shopping experience with designer boutiques tha include Louis Vuitton, Hermès, Gucci, Bottega Veneta, Neiman Marcus, Prada and Jimmy Choo, as well as award-winning cuisine by celebrated chefs; and plenty of outdoor seating areas complete with a fireplace for gathering with friends, two- and four-legged alike

Photos by Julie Clegg

om right: Grace Kelly greets customers at Hepburn; happy hour on the patio at the Heathman Hotel.

ost of the shops welcome dogs cluding Louis Vuitton, Hermès d Salvatore Ferragamo, to name few. Even if you buy nothing, the avern offers beautiful window opping and a luxurious place to ke a stroll with your pooch.

If you'd rather get your exercise e more traditional way, Bellevue home to a number of wonderful stinations for you to explore. owntown Park, a 20-acre oasis green in the heart of Bellevue, atures a promenade, bordered a double row of shade trees, d is a "respite from the activi- es of a busy urban life." There is so a 240-foot wide waterfall that scades into a reflecting pond, mplete with ducks so make sure leash your frisky friend. The -acre lawn offers views of Bel- vue's skyline and Mount Rainier, d is the perfect spot for a picnic ith your pup. Another exercise otion is **Robinswood Off-Leash og Corral**, centrally located in

Bellevue, is a fenced-in, large dog park that offers free parking, complimentary pet waste bags and receptacles, and water spigots for when your pup gets thirsty. If gameplay is more to your liking try the **MetroDemic** game, part scavenger hunt and part trivia challenge, played on your smartphone, where you try to solve as many challenges as possible within the 90-minute timeframe. MetroDemic starts near the Bellevue Transit Station, and after you buy an online ticket a virtual bumbling scientist will lead you and your pup through a series of outbreaks that will have you traveling all over a three-block radius of the city.

If you've saved up all your hunger to enjoy a tasty meal with your pup, Bellevue offers a wide variety of dog-friendly restaurants. One of our recommendations is happy hour at the outdoor garden patio of the **520 Bar and Grill**. If you come to the 520 with a pup you can expect your server to bring a water bowl to quench your dog's thirst. While you can find scrumptious burgers and hot wings, you can also dine on fresh fish, mussels, clams, and steaks. Order the Ahi Tuna Bites that are seared rare with a seaweed garnish and ginger dressing, and the Chicken Avocado Flatbread made with crispy bacon, roasted red peppers, and mozzarella, all topped with chicken and creamy avocado. The ambiance is casual, the food is superb, the service is excellent, and best of all, it's dog friendly.

KIRKLAND Once you're ready to visit a beach, just drive about 15 miles north on I-405 and you'll be in the city of Kirkland. A vibrant waterfront destination, Kirkland is located on the shores of Lake Washington. According to Explore Kirkland (*explorekirkland.com*), no other city in the Puget Sound area has as many waterfront parks and beaches as Kirkland.

If you are looking for an overnight stay, we recommend the pet-friendly **Heathman Hotel**, offering modern luxury in downtown Kirkland. Stay in

Photos by Julie Clegg

Clockwise from top: Relaxing with a glass of Rescue Red at the Heathman; wine tasting at Northwest Cellars; shop dogs Kiwi and Charlie relax at Boo Boo Barkery.

one of the hotel's elegantly appointed Prelude Suites, featuring a king-sized bed with 400 thread sheets, a comfortable seating area, built-in work desk, complimentary WiFi, soaking tub and shower combination, thick terry cloth robes, wet bar, and a large HDTV. Try the Heathman's Furry Friends Getaway Package that includes a doggy bowl, leash with attachable potty bag, plush doggy bed, a special dog treat created by the hotel's Pastry Chef, and a bottle of Heathman Rescue Red private label wine for the humans in the family.

It's a good idea to visit the Heathman's outdoor patio to enjoy a bite to eat before exploring the rest Kirkland has to offer both human and hound. The seasonal menu at the hotel's **Trellis Restaurant**, named one of America's "Top 10 Farm to Table Restaurants," features hand-picked fruits, vegetables and herbs from the executive chef's 18-acre farm. Fresh meat, fish and fowl are sourced from local, artisan producers. Sip on a craft cocktail, made with house-made infusions, on the patio

that's open year around. With a lengthy happy hour from 2-6 p.m. and a menu of delectable items, Trellis at Heathman's is the place to be.

Before you head out to your beach adventures, walk a few blocks to **Booboo Barkery & Boutique** where you and your pooch will enjoy selecting from the doggy goodies, including cakes, cookies, bones, and other assorted goodies. Plus at Booboo you can take advantage of some of the shop's services like grooming, dog training and workshops in addition to offering pet food and accessories. Grab a few treats for your pooch, and maybe even a unique and colorful dog collar made by Squigglechick who creates doggy wear out of upcycled wine labels, beer labels, and candy wrappers.

Stroll along Lake Washington Boulevard and take in the 1.2 mile Lake View Walk by following the blue arrows between downtown Kirkland and **Carillon Point**. On this city hike you'll wind through waterfront parks while seeing whimsical public art. Walk to Marina Park or Carillon Point and rent a kayak or a paddleboard to explore the serene Juanita Bay area of Lake Washington. There are also beach volleyball games going on in the area, feel ee to join in or just watch om a grassy spot on the delines. If you'd rather cycle, ke rentals are also avail- le on the waterfront. Just cure your pooch in a bicycle rrier, and off you go on the **ke Washington Loop**. If you e really adventurous you n tour the entire 62 miles the Loop, or any portion of e Loop by turning around nd pedaling back to Kirkland here you can grab a bite to t after a long afternoon of ercising.

When it's time for a refresh- ent break head to **Flatstick ub**, a craft beer bar and in- oor mini golf course located downtown Kirkland. The ub's 27 rotating taps feature er, wine, and cider made in ashington, plus they offer ersonal size pizzas, baked esh and delivered to your ble through partnership ith nearby restaurants. In e back of the pub, there is a ne-hole mini golf course to allenge any skill level, and hybrid game called duffle- oard that combines mini olf and shuffleboard with a ootball theme. Understand- ly, dogs are not allowed in is area, but they can hang ut nearby, watching a game ith their human on one of e pub's giant flatscreen TVs.

If you prefer grapes over ops, then hop on over to **The rape Choice** and sit at one f the outdoor wine barrel- bles to sip wine and nosh on sty tapas. You and your pup

are also welcome inside The Grape Choice, where there is an expansive shop featuring countless bottles of wines from around the globe as well as Penny's Wine Cave, a private tast- ing room, is also available for small gatherings. Be sure to check out the "cave's" walls, which are lined with recycled wine boxes, providing a cool backdrop for selfies of you and your four-legged companion.

Whether you live in Kirkland or are visiting for the day or weekend, this vibrant, lakeside community of- fers a wide array of places to sit, stay and play with your pooch including **Pickles Playland**, a doggie daycare, indoor dog park and lounge.

From boutiques to barkeries, parks to pubs, you and your furry friend will have plenty to bark about in canine-friendly Kirkland.

Photo by Julie Clegg

Above from left: Wine tasting on the patio at The Grape Choice.

MORE INFORMATION

Hotel Bellevue
11200 SE 6th Street, Bellevue
425.454.4424; thehotelbellevue.com

The Shops at Bravern
11111 NE 8th Street, Bellevue
425.456.8780; thebravern.com

Bellevue Farmers Market
Northwest 6th Street and Compass Plaza
425.454.8474; bellevuefarmersmarket.org

520 Bar and Grill
10146 Main Street, Bellevue
425.450.0520; 520barandgrill.com

The Heathman Hotel
220 Kirkland Avenue, Kirkland
425.284.5800; heathmankirkland.com

Pickles Playland
12669 NE 85th St, Kirkland
425) 298-4530; picklesplayland.dog

Boo Boo Barkery
115 Lake Street South, Kirkland
425.822.0292; booboobarkery.com

Flatstick Pub
15 Lake Street, Kirkland
425.242.1618; flatstickpub.com

The Grape Choice
9 Lakeshore Plaza Dr, Kirkland
425.827.7551; thegrapechoice.com

Northwest Cellars
11909 124th Ave NE, Kirkland
425.825.9463; northwestcellars.com

Juanita Beach Park
9703 NE Juanita Drive, Kirkland

Hepburn
140 Park Lane, Kirkland;
425.576.2730
haleyscottage.mysimplestore.com

Photos by Julie Clegg

Clockwise from top: One of Issaquah Brewery's family of Frog beers; Minnow shows off his new 'do'; signs lead the way to the salmon hatchery; hanging at Issaquah Brewery.

ISSAQUAH Escape to the great outdoors with your dog by heading east on I-90 to explore nearby Issaquah.

Issaquah is surrounded on three sides by the "Issaquah Alps," with Cougar Mountain on the west, Squak Mountain to the south, and Tiger Mountain to the east, forming a natural wonder at the base of the Cascades for boundless opportunities to enjoy outdoor activities with your four-legged friend. Located just 16 miles east of Seattle, it's an easy escape from city life. With the Squak Mountain trailhead conveniently located near downtown Issaquah, first make a pit stop at **Issaquah Brewery**, where frogs appear on the menu...the beer menu, that is. The brewery's family of Frog beers inlcude Menage-a-Frog, Bullfrog Ale, Hippie Frog Chamomile Ale, Grapefruit Frog, Kilted Frog and Wicked Frog to name a few. Acquired by Rogue Ales in 2000, Issaquah Brewery carries Rogue's dog-friendly tradition with annual tasting events such as Frogs & Dogs, and even a menu just for dogs. Items include a Pulled Pork Slider ($2.95) and a classic Peanut Butter and Jelly Sandwich ($3.95).

While at the brewery, it's worth a side trip over to the **Issaquah Salmon Hatchery**, located right next door. Built in 1936, the hatchery annually raises about four million Chinook (King) and Coho (Silver) salmon, which migrate from the Issaquah Creek to Puget Sound, then on to the North Pacific. Stock up on treats at **All the Best**, located at Gilman Village then hit the trails. Combined, Tiger, Cougar and Squak Mountains feature 150 miles of hiking and biking trails, through mostly wooded terrain.

The **Squak Mountain Access Trail** originates at the Issaquah Trail Center parking area (110 SE Bush Street), located near downtown, and follows Issaquah Creek, winding through the foothill neighborhoods until it reaches Sunrise Place, where it enters into more wooded areas and access to Squak Mountain State Park.

If you decide on **Cougar** or **Tiger** for your mountain sojourn, Cougar features almost 50 miles of winding trails, and Tiger (the largest of the three with 13,000 acres of wilderness) features 80 miles of trails. Considered the crown jewel of the Issaquah Alps, Tiger features three peaks, East, West and South. West is considered a favorite among hikers, and can be quite busy with foot and paw traffic on weekends. However, if you are so inclined, take the High Point Way trailhead and follow it to Poo Poo Point (as a dog lover, you have to love the name), one of the country's top hang gliding and paragliding points. Actually, the point got its name from logging signals using a whistle that made a "poo poo" sound. The trail climbs steeply and steadily all the way to the top, but you'll be rewarded with panoramic views of Squak Mountain, Lake Sammamish and Issaquah. There is also a clearing on the backside of the point with an amazing view of Mount Rainier on a clear day.

If hiking isn't your thing, but your hound is in need of some off-leash fun, then **Issaquah Highlands Bark Park** is the spot for Spot. This two-acre dog park is part of the Issaquah Highlands community, which includes over 1,500 acres of parks and open space, a trail that connects directly to the Tiger Mountain complex plus shopping, restaurants and more. Bark Park is located adjacent to Kirk Park on NE Natalie Way and also features a small dog area called Mini-Mutt Meadows.

If you're looking for a romp with Rover in the snow, from the Issaquah Highlands, head east and in just 30 minutes you'll find yourself at the **Summit at Snoqualmie**. While dogs are not allowed on the trail system or in the area around the lodge, if you want to cross country ski or snowshoe with your dog there is the nearby **Gold Creek SnoPark** (from I-90, take Exit 54 to Frontage Road). Dogs on SnoPark trails must be on leash and some areas are shared use, so you may encounter a snowmobile or two.

With its close proximity to Seattle, Issaquah serves as the perfect gateway for you and Fido to escape the hustle and bustle of city life to explore the great outdoors.

A sunny day at the Bark Park.

Photo by Julie Clegg

MORE INFORMATION

Gilman Village
317 NW Gilman Blvd, Issaquah
425.392.6802; gilmanvillage.com

Issaquah Brewery
35 W Sunset Way, Issaquah
425.557.1911; rogue.com

Issaquah Salmon Hatchery
125 W Sunset Way, Issaquah
425.391.9094; issaquahfish.org

Issaquah Highlands Bark Park
Located on NE Natalie Way

Squak Mountain Access Trail
110 SE Bush Street; www.ci.issaquah.wa.us

Gold Creek SnoPark
I-90 to Exit 54 to Frontage Road
www.parks.wa.gov/winter/trails/

Photos by Amelia Soper

Clockwise from top: Enjoying the view of Snoqualmie Fall; signature Salish dog biscuits; stay warm with a Salish fleece blanket; kick back with your canine in a Salish terry robe.

SNOQUALMIE FALLS Located just 30 miles from Seattle, is the **Salish Lodge & Spa**, perched above the spectacular, 268 feet high Snoqualmie Falls—it's a special place for relaxation and rejuvenation, and pampering for human and canine alike.

The Lodge is truly a quintessential Pacific Northwest experience, with 86 luxurious retreat-like guestrooms each with their own gas fireplaces, spa-style showers, oversized soaking tubs, and view of the mighty Snoqualmie River. The Lodge has soaring ceilings, rich, warm wood beams and tables, and is home to a world-class spa that specializes in creating treatments with herbs and honey cultivated onsite.

Your fuzzy buddy will love staying at the Lodge, where they offer the **Pampered Paws Package**, "the ultimate in doggy relaxation!" Your dog will drool over the Pampered Paws goodies just waiting to be discovered, including all-natural bee-shaped doggy treats, a comfy Salish Lodge & Spa dog blanket for you to take home, and a lovely bone shaped ID tag for your dog to always remember his time at the Lodge. Humans do pretty well too at the Lodge, with their very own super soft, terry cloth bathrobes perfect for sinking into the luxurious featherbed, complete with high-end linens and six varieties of pillows to choose from. Your room is also home to a very large HD flat panel television, mini fridge, lavender mint bath amenities, coffee services, a newspaper delivered daily during your stay, and complimentary WiFi. There's so much to enjoy in your room it might be hard to get out and explore, but do try! Note: Well behaved dogs are welcome to stay alone in Lodge rooms.

For exploring around the grounds of the Lodge, take a stroll along the heath

-lined path to enjoy the stunning
ews of the 268-foot high **Sno-
ualmie Falls**. Prepare to be awed
the falls are 100 feet taller than
iagra Falls. You can walk out to
observation for an even more
ectacular view. No matter if it's
nny, prepare to get a little wet
hen you visit Snoqualmie Falls
the mist of the pounding water
tting the rocks below floats all
ound, leaving everything just a
tle damp. The area also features
two-acre park with an enjoyable
e mile round-trip hike that fol-
ws the River Trail through trees
d open slopes, ending with a
autiful view of the Falls. Make
re to stop at the gift shop where
u can get some of the infamous
noqualmie Falls pancake mix to
ake at home.

When hunger strikes, head to
e Lodge's **Attic Lounge**. Casual
nd comfortable, it features a stone
earth pizza oven, cozy furniture
nd a fireplace to kick-back and
lax. Bar offerings include Hive
ive Hopped Honey Ale produced
y Pike Brewing Company, Salish
oney-flavored vodka and private
bel wines. The menu features
andcrafted pizzas and sandwich-
s fired in the artisan pizza oven.
Vhether you're looking for a light
nack, a glass of wine from the
unge's wide-ranging selection, or
place to enjoy a favorite cocktail,
e Attic is the perfect place to sit
ack and take in the breathtaking
iews of the Snoqualmie Valley.

For a bit more formal fare, the
alish Lodge is reknowned for
ts cuisine where menu choices
nclude starting with a delicious
ed wine blend, paired with a kale

and baby gem lettuce salad that includes
apples, pecans, goat cheese and pome-
granate vinaigrette; followed by roasted
scallops with chestnuts and porcini
mushrooms. Save room as your main
course is coming, a crispy roasted duck
leg, with braised red cabbage, smoked
bacon, dates and Salish honey port jus.

Speaking of honey, another surprise
is the Lodge's own honey bee apiary,
which produces over 2,400 pounds of
honey per year. Inspired by the need to
provide bees a sustainable environment
in which to thrive, the Lodge planted a
hillside of wildflowers that lead up to
the apiary and gardens, along with blueberry and huckleberry plants. When you
walk around the area, look for the Salish
bee to guide you to items that feature the
lodge's honey, like their restaurant cui-
sine, the honey-based treatments in The Spa, honey-ale beer, honey-infused
vodka, and even honey truffles.

Photos by Amelia Soper

**From top: Pausing to appreciate
the little touches along the trail;
Thya dons her bone-shaped tag,
compliments of Salish Lodge.**

Not to be forgotten, Salish Lodge offers your furry friend his own delectable meal from the Canine Cuisine In-Room Dining Menu. Prepared in-house
by the lodge's own culinary staff, menu items include gourmet specialties
such as Hens Fit for a Hound, made with organic chicken breast, baby carrots,
green beans, chicken jelly and Arborio rice, Pescetarian Pooch, with wild

Photos by Amelia Soper

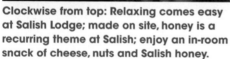

Clockwise from top: Relaxing comes easy at Salish Lodge; made on site, honey is a recurring theme at Salish; enjoy an in-room snack of cheese, nuts and Salish honey.

upper falls. The trail continues one more mile to connect with the old Milwaukee Railroad trail in **Iron Horse State Park**. It's a great way to start the morning. If you are feeling a bit more adventurous, another popular hike is traversing the switchback to reach **Rattlesnake Ledge**. The 1700' vertical climb is over two miles and will certainly raise the heart rate human and canine alike. Once you reach the top, be extremely careful, as the ledge is 400 to 500 feet down on three sides.

If your pup needs to get some running in, we've got you covered. The **Three Forks Natural Area** has more than 200 acres of open space situated at the confluence of the south fork, north fork and middle fork of the Snoqualmie River, with an astounding up-close view of Mount Si. Adjacent to the natural area is the Three Forks Off-Leash Dog Park, the only designated off-leash park in the upper valley. It features eight acres of open space for off-leash fun including water access.

Post a morning of exercise, head to **Piccola Cellar** in North Bend, a dog-friendly wine bar located inside an old fire station, with a roll up garage doors and a custom bar made from reclaimed timber. With eight wines on tap, you can

salmon, plump quinoa, and steamed corn and peas, and classic Meat and Potatoes made with juicy roast beef, roasted potatoes, steamed baby carrots, all smothered with beef gravy. See, you can take care of everyone when you stay at the Lodge—and then pack it in for a good night's rest as tomorrow brings a lot more to explore.

Waking up later than normal happens when you stay at Salish Lodge, it has that mystical pull that makes you want to hit the snooze button and stay in bed a little bit longer. Once you do rise and get a tasty breakfast under your belt, it's time to walk the pup and see what the area has to offer. We suggest a trip to **Twin Falls State Park** in nearby North Bend. The Park's trail extends 1.25 miles from North Bend to Twin Falls. Just before the first footbridge, steps descend to a breathtaking viewpoint of the lower falls, and just past the footbridge is another viewpoint of the

ajoy a glass, get a growler go, or purchase a wine te filled with your favorite end to enjoy on your next utdoor adventure or back at e Lodge. Not forgetting your up, nearby **Pet Place Market**, as plenty of plush toys, cool ccessories, and wholesome od and treats. While there, ke advantage of the convenient self-wash stations to get our soggy doggy looking and melling fresh again.

On your way back to the odge, swing into **Bindlestick offeehouse and Bar**, a local angout that welcomes dogs. ry the the Emporer of the orth sandwich stuffed with a ariety of deli meat, provolone

Just outside the dog-friendly rooms, is a fully-fenced garden area.

neese, and topped with Tuscan Italian dressing. ou can sip a cold pint of Northwest beer while our pup munches on the goodies you purchased arlier. On weekends, the Bindlestick becomes popular venue for live music, fire-spinners, npromptu grill outs, and other fun events, plus e outdoor firepit is the perfect place to enjoy a ld one with your canine companion.

Once back at the Lodge, check out **The Spa**, hich features a eucalyptus steam room, dry auna and therapeutic soaking pool; and a menu f seemingly endless rejuvenating body and skin eatments including the Salish Signature Heated iver Rock Massage, a variety of facials, or "Rain rop Therapy," which features "a combination f aromatherapy essential oils that are dispensed ke rain drops along the spine and gently ispersed to stimulate nerves using techniques at will bring balance to your body from head toe." Can't choose? If you have time, then try few. Between the friendly staff, delicious food, ll-service spa, in-room amenities, Snoqualmie alls, and so much more, you'll leave Salish odge relaxed and rejuvenated! 🐾

MORE INFORMATION

Salish Lodge & Spa
6501 Railroad Avenue SE, Snoqualmie
800.2.SALISH (800.272.5474); salishlodge.com

Piccola Cellars
112 West 2nd Street
North Bend, Wash.
425.486.9463; piccolawine.com

The Bindlestick Coffeehouse and Bar
7822 Douglas Avenue SE
Snoqualmie, Wash.
425.888.0259

Three Forks Off-Leash Dog Park
39912 SE Park Street
Snoqualmie, Wash.

Pet Place Market
213 Bendigo Blvd N Ste 2
North Bend, Wash.
425.888.8828; petplacemarket.com

Photo by Amelia Soper

Photos by Amelia Soper

Clockwise from top: Buckley Brown with his ball at Waters; Nine Hats serves up some tasty wine; listen to vinyl while sipping wine at Sleight of Hand; hanging with Leia at Nine Hats Wine.

SODO Wineries

SODO IS HOME TO STADIUMS, STARBUCKS AND WINERIES... LOTS OF DOG-FRIENDLY WINERIES!

PATTERSON CELLARS Upon arrival at **Patterson Cellars**, we are greeted by winery dog Hamilton. Typically hanging out at the Woodinville location it's a treat to meet the seven-year-old Labrador-mix. Founded in 2000 by owner and winemaker John Patterson, Patterson Cellars creates a wide variety of wines, including robust red blends, elegant single varietals, classic whites, lively rosés, sparkling wines and lush dessert wines. With four different tasting rooms in Woodinville, Eastern Washington, Leavenworth, and SODO, their new SODO tasting room brings wine country to Seattle in a modern lofty space with outdoor seating, perfec for bringing your dog along on your urban wine tasting adventure. To learn more, visit **pattersoncellars.com**.

NINE HATS WINES Next, we move on to **Nine Hats Wines**, where our model, nine-month-old husky Leia is ready for her photo shoot. Launched in 2007, Nine Hats was inspired by Long Shadows' team of nine internationally renowned vintners. It started with just one Nine Hats wine, a red blend. The overwhelming success of the red lead to the expansion of the brand, and Nine Hats has come out of the shadows to assemble a portfolio of nine uniquely sophisticated wines (we recommend th 2016 Cabernet Sauvignon). Their new SODO tasting room is the perfect place to take your dog for a fun outing—es-

ecially because it adoins **Nine Pies
zzeria**, owned and operated by
lebrated pizzaiolo Cary Kemp.
parated by a large sliding glass
oor, you can order one of their de-
ious, New York-style pizzas (we
commend the Piaggio, accompa-
ed by an arugala salad) and have
served on the dog-friendly patio
delivered to Nine Hats Wines.
or more information, visit **nine-
atswines.com** and **ninepiespizza.
m**.

ATERS WINERY Specializing in
eating exclusive and unique red
ines, **Waters Winery** is the place
go for red wine lovers and their
gs. As we enter the tasting room,
uckley Brown is there to greet us,
ith ball in mouth. We are told
ght-year-old Buckley used to live
the vineyard in Walla Walla and
now learning how to be a city
g — but, as we set up for our pho-
shoot, we find him to be quite the
ell-mannered gentleman. Founded
2005 in Walla Walla, their red
ines rival the finest of the Old and
ew World regions. They produce
eir wines in small batches — just
few thousand cases a year — to
ing each person who tastes it an
xperience they won't soon forget. If
u find yourself in SODO with your dog and a hanker-
g for some great red wine, check out Waters' tasting
om. For more information, visit **trwines.com**.

Photos by Amelia Soper

**Clockwise from top: Sweet Hamilton
was happy to pose for the camera
while we enjoy a tasting at Patterson;
Leia lounging at Sleight of Hand; one
of our favorite wines, Structure.**

LEIGHT OF HAND **Sleight of Hand Cellars** was
unded in 2007 by winemakers Trey Busch and Jerry
d Sandy Solomon. In its short lifetime, Sleight of
and has been named one of "The Next Generation"
up-and-coming wineries in Washington by Seattle
agazine, and is known for creating world-class wines
fit any palate. Their SODO tasting room opened in
16, and is the perfect spot to bring your dog, sip on
me wine, and listen to great music. **sofhcellars.com**

KERLOO CELLARS
With a new tasting room in SODO, this Walla Walla-
founded winery is known for creating unique wines
that will challenge and spark your palate. Ryan Crane,
the winemaker, got his start as a volunteer at Animale
Wine Cellars in Seattle, where he fell in love with the
process of creating and crafting wine, and opened
Kerloo Cellars in 2007. In 2015, Crane moved Kerloo
from Walla Walla to SODO, where he's been attracting
people and their dogs ever since. Well-behaved pups
are always welcome! **kerloocellars.com**

Photo by Amelia Soper

STRUCTURE CELLARS From a humble basement in their Ballard home to the SODO space it occupies today, **Structure Cellars** is a true gem in the SODO wine district (and so is their Boston terrier, Valentine, pictured above). Founded in 2014 by Brian Grasso and Brandee Slosar, this married couple took their dream of owning a winery and made it a reality. Through hard work, perseverance, and education, they opened not one, but two tasting rooms at SODO (The Blueprint Room and the Cellar Room), where they bring their unique white and red wines to the public (our favorite is the 2016 Cabernet Franc). They welcome pups of all sizes with open arms at both tasting rooms—slobbery kisses included! For more information, visit **structurewines.com.**

LATTA WINES If you like small-batch unique wines, then **Latta Wines** is for you. One of our favorites, Latta was founded in 2011 by owner and winemaker Andrew Latta, who brings his customers uncommon and unique varietals from the most unique vineyards of Washington state. In addition to showcasing small-batch wines, they love having doggy visitors to their SODO tasting room. While you sip on wine, they can sip on water and enjoy pats and scratches from other wine-drinking dog lovers like you! Visit their website at **lattawines.com.**

SCHOONERS EXACT BREWING COMPANY While not exactly a winery, it's worth mentioning **Schooner EXACT Brewing Company**, founded in 2006 by three beer-obsessed friends experimenting with home brew in a garage. It wasn't until 2012 that their dream was entirely realized with a family-friendly brewery and restaurant in SODO. Beers include Evergreen IPA, Hopvine IPA, Emerald ISA, Hopferno Black IPA, First Session ISA, and Snowpacolypse Black ISA. Well-behaved dogs are welcome on the outdoor patio during warm weather (or whenever the patio is open). Check out their menu at **schoonerexact.com.**

To visit any of these awesome establishments, head to **SODO Urban Works** at 3931 1st Ave S in Seattle and spend the day sipping wine with your furry friend. 🐾

Above: Valentine strikes a pose at Structure Cellar

MELIA SOPER
HOTOGRAPHY
Mfriendtographer

EDDING +
ENGAGEMENT
HOTOGRAPHY

r couples who *love* their dogs.

melia soper, *your* friendtographer
follow me: @yourfriendtographer
d me a text: 206.954.9449
p me a line: amelia@soperphotography.com
it me: **www.soperphotography.com**

NTION YOU FOUND US HERE IN CITYDOG AND GET
% OFF YOUR 2019 OR 2020 WEDDING COLLECTION!

NOW BOOKING
THROUGH 2020

PATTERSON
CELLARS

HOLLYWOOD HILL TASTING ROOM
WOODINVILLE, WA

———

**WAREHOUSE DISTRICT WINERY
& TASTING ROOM**
WOODINVILLE, WA

———

SEATTLE SODO TASTING ROOM
SEATTLE, WA

———

LEAVENWORTH TASTING ROOM
LEAVENWORTH, WA

EXPLORE
WASHINGTON WINE.

START HERE.

PATTERSONCELLARS.COM

Photo by Amelia Soper

Deluxe Digs

WE'VE DUG UP SOME SUPER
SWANKY PLACES FOR YOU AND
FIDO TO STAY IN THE SEATTLE AREA.

Palladian Hotel 🐾 🐾 🐾 🐾
2000 2nd Avenue, Seattle
206.448.1111; palladianhotel.com

Hotel Sorrento 🐾 🐾 🐾 🐾
900 Madison Street, Seattle
206.622.6400; hotelsorrento.com

Edgewater Hotel 🐾 🐾 🐾 🐾
2411 Alaskan Way, Seattle
206.728.7000; edgewaterhotel.com

W Seattle 🐾 🐾 🐾 🐾
1112 4th Ave, Seattle
206.264.6000; marriott.com/hotels/
travel/seawh-w-seattle

Woodmark Hotel 🐾 🐾 🐾 🐾
1200 Carillon Point, Kirkland
425. 822.3700; destinationhotels.
com/the-woodmark

Pictured here: The Palladian.

Fairmont Olympic Hotel 🐾 🐾 🐾 🐾
411 University Street, Seattle,
206.621.1700; fairmont.com/seattle

Hotel Monaco 🐾 🐾 🐾 🐾
1101 4th Avenue, Seattle
206.621.1770; monaco-seattle.com

Hotel Max 🐾 🐾 🐾 🐾
620 Stewart Street,
206.728.6299; hotelmaxseattle.com

Hotel Vintage 🐾 🐾 🐾 🐾
1100 5th Avenue, Seattle
206.624.8000; hotelvintage-seattle.com

Alexis Hotel 🐾 🐾 🐾 🐾
1007 1st Avenue, Seattle
206.624.4844; alexishotel.com

Motif Seattle 🐾 🐾 🐾 🐾
1415 5th Avenue, Seattle
206.971.8000; destinationhotels.
com/motif-seattle

Maxwell Hotel 🐾 🐾 🐾
300 Roy Street, Seattle
877.298.9728; staypineapple.com/
the-maxwell-hotel-seattle-wa

Pan Pacific 🐾 🐾 🐾 🐾
2125 Terry Avenue, Seattle
206.264.8111; panpacificseattle.com

Four Seasons Hotel 🐾 🐾 🐾 🐾
99 Union Street, Seattle
206.749.7000; fourseasons.com

Hotel 1000 🐾 🐾 🐾 🐾
1000 1st Avenue, Seattle
206.957.1000; loewshotels.com/
hotel-1000-seattle

Heathman Hotel 🐾 🐾 🐾 🐾
220 Kirkland Avenue, Kirkland
425.284.5800; heathmankirkland.co

Hotel Five 🐾 🐾 🐾
2200 5th Avenue, Seattle
206.441.9785; staypineapple.com/
hotel-five-seattle-wa

Cedarbrook Lodge 🐾 🐾 🐾
18525 36th Avenue S, Seattle
206.901.9268; cedarbrooklodge.con

Hotel Andra 🐾 🐾 🐾 🐾
2000 Fourth Avenue, Seattle
206.448.8600; hotelandra.com

Photo by Ameila Soper

Off-Leash Dog Parks

SEATTLE + KING COUNTY

Carkeek Park
950 NW Carkeek Park Road, Seattle

Golden Gardens Dog Park
8498 Seaview Place NW, Seattle

Warren G. Magnuson Park
NW 74th Street, Seattle

Westcrest Park
9000 8th Avenue SW, Seattle

Blue Dog Pond
1520 26th Avenue S, Seattle

Denny Park
100 Dexter Ave N, Seattle

Dr. Jose Rizal
1007 12th Avenue S, Seattle,

I-5 Colonnade
1701 Lakeview Boulevard E, Seattle
Lower Kinnear
870 Elliott Avenue W, Seattle

Magnolia Manor
3500 28th Avenue W, Seattle

Northacres
12718 1st Avenue NE, Seattle

Plymouth Pillars
1050 Pike Street, Seattle

Regrade Park
2251 3rd Avenue, Seattle

Woodland Off-Leash Area
1000 N 50th Street, Seattle

Beaver Lake Dog Park
2600 244th Avenue SE, Sammamish

Next page: Enjoying a sunny day at Warren G. Magnuson Park.

Marymoor Park
6046 W Lake Sammamish Parkway NE, Redmond

Cedar River Dog Park
1717 SE Maple Valley Hwy, Renton

French Lake Dog Park
33325 8th Avenue S, Federal Way

Genesee Park Off Leash Area
4513 S Genesee Street, Seattle

Jasper's Dog Park
11301 NE 120th Street, Kirkland

Luther Burbank Dog Park
2040 84th Avenue SE, Mercer Island

Edmonds Beach Dog Park
498 Admiral Way, Edmonds

Richmond Beach Saltwater Park
2021 Northwest 190th Street, Seattle

Robinswood Park
151st Place SE, Bellevue

Strawberry Hill Dog Park
7666 Northeast High School Rd
Bainbridge Island

Three Forks Dog Park
39903 SE Park Street, Snoqualmie

SNOHOMISH COUNTY

Cavelero Off Leash Dog Park
7900 20th Street SE, Lake Stevens

Eagle Park
701 E. Galena Street, Granite Falls

Howarth Park
1127 Olympic Boulevard, Everett

Loganberry Lane Off-Leash Area
18th Avenue W, Everett

Lowell Off Leash Dog Park
4605 S 3rd Avenue, Everett

Mountlake Terrace Dog Park
5303 228th Street SW
Mountlake Terrace

Strawberry Fields
6100 152nd Street NE, Marysville

Tambark Creek Park
17217 35th Avenue SE, Bothell

Willis D. Tucker Community Park
6705 Puget Park Drive, Snohomish

Lake Stickney Park
13521 Manor Way, Lynnwood

Osprey Park
707 First Street, Sultan

TACOMA + PIERCE COUNTY

Chambers Bay Off Leash Park
6320 Grandview Drive W, Tacoma

Clarks Creek Park
1700 12th Avenue SW, Puyallup

Dacca Park
2820 54th Avenue E, Tacoma

Fort Steilacoom Off-Leash Area
8698 87th Avenue SW, Lakewood

French Lake Dog Park
31531 1st Avenue S, Federal Way

PenMet Rotary Bark Park
10100 Bujacich Rd NW, Gig Harbor

Point Defiance Off Leash Area
Five Mile Road, Tacoma

Rogers Dog Park
3300 East L Street, Tacoma

Viking Park, Off-leash Dog Park
82nd Street E, Bonney Lake

Wapato Lake Off-Leash Dog Park
6500 S Sheridan Avenue, Tacoma

Wright Park
501 South I Street, Tacoma

THURSTON COUNTY

Hawk's Prairie Dog Park
2420 Hogum Bay Road NE, Lacey

Shelton Off-Leash Dog Area
100 Turner Avenue, Shelton

ISLAND COUNTY

Double Bluff Beach
S Double Bluff Road, Freeland

Photo by Julie Clegg

Tacoma & South Puget Sound

Known for its world-renowned glass art, Tacoma's vibrant urban core is bustling, with plenty of places to sit, stay and play.

Photo by Brandie Ahlgren

Best Friend Photography

portraits of your dog or cat

by

Emily Rieman

www.bestfriendphoto.com

206-935-5624

gift certificates available

Give the gift that has tails wagging!

CityDog, the definitive dog lover's magazine about life and living with dogs in the West.

Subscribe at
citydogmagazine.com

Holly C. Cook Photography

Commercial and Private Pet Photography
www.hollyccook.com
(425) 239-3768

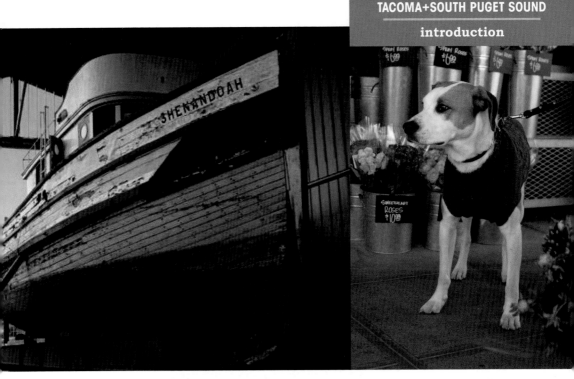

JUST AN HOUR SOUTH OF SEATTLE AND TWO HOURS NORTH OF PORTLAND, THE SOUTH PUGET SOUND AREA IS HOME TO A LOT OF HIDDEN DOG-FRIENDLY GEMS.

The South Sound region is a warm and welcoming place, home to a plethora of cities, towns, hamlets, and best of all crystal clear water and lush greenery. There are so many stops along the South Sound area, with no two alike, that you can spend weeks, if not months, exploring the area. Boat exploration and kayak camping are well practiced sports in the South Sound, but if you want to explore by car, bus, train, or even bicycle, it can be done in this region. The two must-see places for dog lovers, in addition to the trendy city of Tacoma, are Gig Harbor, and the Washington state capital city of Olympia.

If you go by train, Amtrak is dog-friendly...sort of...for a fee, they welcome dogs up to 20 pounds. This is good news for those of us with small dogs who routinely take trips on the Coach Starlight which travels between Vancouver, B.C. and Los Angeles, with numerous stops in between including Tacoma, Olympia and Portland.

No matter how you get there, Tacoma is revived and ready to welcome you and your pup with open arms. Explore the **Point Defiance**

above from right: The Harbor History Museum in Gig Harbor; shopping for flowers at Metropolitan Market in Tacoma.

Zoo and Aquarium where you can see a Wild West-themed outdoor theater that features "Sheruff' Bones, also known as Herald the dog, and a host of other animals having fun showing guests how to reduce, reuse, and recycle. In Gig Harbor, take a walk through the **Harbor History Museum** to see regional maritime relics and in Olympia, a tour of the capitol campus is a must.

These free, 50-minute, guided tours explore portions of the 250,000 square-foot capitol building, including the 175-foot tall dome made of 33,000 pounds of brick; as well as the capitol's well manicured grounds, and legislative areas. The history is rich in the South Sound, and you can explore it with your best friend by your side.

Harbor History Museum photo courtesy of Travel Tacoma

Tacoma

KNOWN FOR ITS GLASS ART, TACOMA'S VIBRANT URBAN CORE IS ALIVE WITH CULTURE.

STAY When visiting Tacoma, we like to stay at **Hotel Murano** for its convenient, downtown location. Artistic in style, reflecting Tacoma's place in glass art, the Murano is just steps from the Tacoma Convention Center and a few blocks from Tacoma's best museums and restaurants. Orizon, a monumental 75-foot-tall curved steel and plate glass sculpture welcomes you to the Murano, and don't forget to look skyward in the lobby to see three giant stained glass Viking boats suspended as if gliding through air. The glass theme carries throughout the Murano, including guest rooms and you can even enjoy a docent-led tour of the artwork.

The Murano loves dogs, and provides your pup with a a pet bed, water and food bowls, and a tasty pup treat upon arrival, and they even have a list of Tacoma pet resources for you to visit while in town. Guest rooms are large at the Murano, and come with a plush king-size bed, or two double beds, a range of speciality sleeping pillows, luxurious bathrobes, spa-like bathroom, locally infused honor bar, coffee and tea bar, a large HDTV, bluetooth clock radio, and complimentary WiFi. There is also a 24-hour gym and business center available for guests.

Once checked in, and all of your pup's amenities stored away, it's time to hit the town with your

Clockwise from top: Dakota takes it easy in the Murano's grand entrance; the inviting exterior of the hotel; experience innovative fine dining and fine art at Bite; the show-stopping, all glass wall-scape by artist Janusz Walentynowicz; Dutch artist Vebeke's glass viking ships.

Photo by Nichole Sears

ound. Leash up your pup and get ready to be amazed. Walking from the otel, head southeast for the 15 minute walk to the **Chihuly Bridge of Glass** etween Dock Street and Pacific Avenue.

Typically, viewing artist Dale Chihuly's pieces of art is a costly museum xperience, but in 2002 Chihuly, a Tacoma native, was commissioned to reate artwork that the Museum of Glass would give to the city of Tacoma. hus the Bridge of Glass was designed, a 500-foot-long pedestrian bridge hat links downtown Tacoma to the Thea Foss Waterway. The Chihuly ridge of Glass is glorious, and easily explored with your pup in tow.

Free and accessible 24-hours a day, the Bridge starts closest to the down-own core with a covered pavilion, home to nearly 2,500 pieces of aquatic aspired glass pieces hanging down from overhead, and it continues on the edestrian bridge, each section showcasing fine glass art. You and your pup ill spend a lot of time walking back and forth, looking at the displays, and vatching how the sunlight, or moonlight depending upon when you visit, lays upon the different colors, shapes, and sizes of the glass.

LAY Another really awe-inspiring place to visit in Tacoma is **Point efiance Park**, the largest park in Pierce County. Point Defiance Park is ome to 760 acres that traverse a national forest and saltwater beaches, plus ouses a zoo, an aquarium, a conservatory, and a nature center. With all of his expansive land, Point Defiance devoted 7-acres to an off-leash dog park or pups of all sizes, and it even includes a small dog area for the wee pups. here are three parking lots located at the off-leash area, or you can park at he Fort Nisqually Picnic Area for a walk prior to pup play in the dog park.

bove from left: Glass art installation at Union Station; surrounded y downtown Tacoma, Hotel Murano is a city dog's delight.

SIT With all of the amazing things accomplished in day one of your stay, it's definitely time to eat. For scrumptious food, with a dog-friendly atmosphere, we highly recommend **Engine House No. 9**. Housed in the original firehouse number 9 that was built in 1907, the Engine House originally served as the battalion headquarters, and protected the north end of Tacoma. Today the Engine House is listed on the National Register of Historic Places and throws down great eats, divine drinks, and has expanded to include its own brewery. Walking into the Engine House you'll be greeted by dog-loving people, and seated in the large outside area that has shaded and non-shaded areas. Fido will be given a bowl of fresh water leaving you free to peruse the menu, which is good news because the Engine House has a lot to offer. Miss your mom's cooking?

Clockwise from top: Dakota is a fan of
the hotel's luxurious linens; the historic
Pantages Theater; Hotel Murano has
carefully curated a collection of 20th-
century works in glass.

Then try Not Your Mama's Meatloaf. Made with bacon and beef, roasted garlic, Yukon mashed potatoes, and caramelized onions, this meatloaf will stick to your ribs, and maybe even your shirt! You might also want to try the Country Fried Wagyu Steak, fish tacos, Backdraft Barbeque Pork sandwich, or their Famous Firehouse Chili. Whatever you decide to chow down on, quench your thirst with the Engine House's own Belgian White Witbier Session Ale.

For a couple of other pup-loving eateries, you can check out **Top of Tacoma Bar & Café** where they specialize in pork belly, fish, wraps, and southwest fare, and even offer truly delicious vegan alternatives; and **Hank's Bar and Grill**, a true neighborhood restaurant offering 21 beers and ciders on tap, homemade fresh pretzels, tasty pizzas made-to-order, and hot and cold sandwiches.

PLAY After enjoying your meal, you'll probably want to lay down but don't do that! Make your way to Ruston Way waterfront where you will be enamored.

Ruston Way has a two-mile paved scenic waterfront walkway that offers glorious views of Commencement Bay, one of the southernmost spots of the Puget Sound. A stroll along the path is great for people watching, or if you're feeling up to a little jog or rollerblading with your pooch.

Kayaking is also readily available out of this beautiful area as is fishing, and if you feel up to it you can rent a pedal powered surrey with a fringe on top from **Wheel Fun Rentals** and pedal your pooch up and down the boulevard!

With a good day of fun and entertainment under your belt, it's time to head on back to the Murano for a bubbly soak in the marble tub, along with a nice tasty glass of wine. When you've soaked all your cares away, head down to **Bite**, the hotel's restaurant or order room service. We recommend the fried green tomatoes, corn and crab chowder, and cedar plank wild salmon with fingerling potatoes. Yum!

SIT Waking up refreshed and ready to go, make haste to **Mad Hat Tea Company**. Mad Hat is "an urban tea house in the heart of Tacoma," and offers teas in all assorted flavors including black, green, white, chai, botanical, oolong, rooibos, yerba mate, and a variety of blends guaranteed to soothe your soul.

If coffee is more to your liking then head northwest a few blocks to **Bluebeard Coffee Roasters**.

Awake? Check! Okay, it's time to head to the **Proctor District**.

Murano photos by Nichole Sears; Pantages Theater photo courtesy of Travel Tacoma

n most Saturdays, the **Proctor Farmers Market** is open and dogs are elcome. Wander past vendors selling an array of fruits, veggies, and other oodies, while listening to the sounds of talented local musicians. Meal me is easy at the market, with homemade tamales, empanadas, tandoori, nd smoothies. Remember to bring a few treats for your pooch and stay r the day. Speaking of treats, you can stock up at **Next to Nature**, an dependently owned pet store, located in the heart of downtown Tacoma.

LAY Heading south, be sure to visit **Fort Steilacoom Park,** a massive 340- cre park, located in nearby Lakewood. There's a 22-acre off-leash area, with pecial areas for dogs big and small, numerous walking trails, places for ur pooch to get water, and poop scoop bags. 🐾

ORE INFORMATION

otel Murano
20 Broadway, Tacoma
3.238.8000; hotelmuranotacoma.com

ext to Nature
39 Tacoma Avenue S, Tacoma
3) 779-8141; next-to-nature.com

uebeard Coffee Roasters
01 6th Avenue, Tacoma
3.272-5600; bluebeardcoffee.com

ad Hat Tea Company
30 Commerce Street, Tacoma
3.441.2111; madhattea.com

Engine House No. 9
611 N Pine Street, Tacoma
253.272.3435; ehouse9.com

Top of Tacoma Bar & Café
3529 McKinley Avenue, Tacoma
253.272.1502

Point Defiance Park
5400 N Pearl Street, Tacoma

Fort Steilacoom Park
8714 87th Avenue SW, Lakewood

Photos courtesy of Travel Tacoma and Pierce County

Clockwise from above: DuPont backdropped by Mount Rainier; Mount Rainier and Myrtle Falls in Pierce County; enjoying a stroll through Fort Steilacoom Park.

Photos by Holly Cook

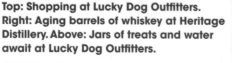

**Top: Shopping at Lucky Dog Outfitters.
Right: Aging barrels of whiskey at Heritage
Distillery. Above: Jars of treats and water
await at Lucky Dog Outfitters.**

GETTING HERE Take I-5 S for approximately 20 miles. Take exit 132 toward WA-16 W.
Keep right at the fork to Exit 132B. Follow signs for Gig Harbor/Bremerton/WA-16 W.
Keep left onto WA-16 W. Take the Wollochet Dr NW exit toward City Center.

Gig Harbor

DISCOVER, EAT, STAY AND PLAY
IN SOUTH PUGET SOUND'S
BEAUTIFUL GIG HARBOR.

GIG HARBOR Wandering the
waterfront in **Gig Harbor**, one
can see that it once was a robust
fishing village. While you can sti
find fishing boats anchored in the
harbor, and witness the Blessing
of the Fleet that occurs every yea
the town is evolving into a destination worth exploring in search
of adventure with your dog.

PLAY Start your adventure at **Ro
tary Bark Park**, the local Gig Ha
bor dog park. Rotary Bark Park
is 97-acres of forest and trails,
with a 15-acre off-leash dog area
that is equipped and maintained
by CHEW Dog Rescue. Park at
the Fire District #5 Headquarters
where you can head down a trai
to the park. Don't forget to fill up
your water bottle at the trailhead
spigot so you and your pup don'
get parched. You'll know you've
arrived at the Bark Park when yo
come to the fenced-in area with
a double gated entry. Tall trees
provide ample shade for you to
rest and enjoy the lushness of the
park. If you feel like hiking, there
are trails that cut through the glo
rious forest. You can spend hour
at Bark Park, and it's a great plac
to get your dog's daily exercise.

After your romp, head to the
Gourmet Burger Shop, where
dogs are welcome on the deck.

bove, from top: **Fergie gazes out the window at the dog-friendly Wesley n; Lucky Dog Outfitters provides cool gear for Gig Harbor dogs.**

When you are ready to explore make sure your next stop has your g in mind. **Lucky Dog Outfitters** is everything a pet store should : great gear for dogs plus friendly and knowledgeable staff. Lucky g carries a variety of outdoor dog gear, including "pup tents," ats in all shapes, sizes and flavors, colorful leashes, bath-time odies and party bakery items. Another must stop is **Green Cottage ts,** which specializes in locally-made products and has a robust of-ring of nutritious pet food. Green Cottage Pets owner, Tom Moodie, a former chef with a focus on bringing his customers high-quality redients. Either or both of these pet stores offer wonderful goodies r your dog to munch.

Another dog-friendly stop is **Tickled Pink** to quench your desire r some fun and fashion. While Tickled Pink does offer sweaters, ps, and accessories in pink, it offers items in an array of colors and en has their own line of scarves, handbags and jewelry. Make sure get a doggy treat from one of the store's employees.

What's better than a little libation after some retail thera-py? Across the street from Tick-led Pink you'll find **Heritage Distilling Company**, where you can taste their whiskey and bourbon that is aged onsite in wood barrels. Heritage is the most awarded craft distillery in North America by the Ameri-can Distilling Institute five years in a row—and partnered with Pearl Jam to produce a special edition brown sugar bourbon, raising over $100,000 to help end homelessness.

When it's coffee time, head to **Java and Clay**, where you can get a great cup of joe. There is an outdoor deck with an amaz-ing view of the harbor for you to enjoy your caffeine and rest up. Dogs are also welcome in the ceramic studio, where you can select from pre-sculpted coffee cups, spoon rests, night lights, and other items to paint, fire, and take home. The staff will explain the entire process and show you painting techniques to help you create a work of art.

STAY After a big day out on the lovely town of Gig Harbor, it's time to find a place to stay for the night and for that we recommend the **Wesley Inn**. Upon arrival at the Wesley Inn you'll be met by their new four-legged greeter, Wesley. Wesley has some big paws to fill and is training to take on the role of his predecessor Patrick, who passed away and is greatly missed. To learn more about Patrick visit the Inn's Fireplace Room where his photo sits prominently next to a memorial dedicated to him.

Above: Gig Harbor's lovely and dog-friendly Best Western Wesley Inn & Suites.

As you can guess, the Wesley Inn, a Best Western property, is dog-friendly, and that's great news as you both will enjoy the simple and relaxing décor, and amenities that include free WiFi, a morning paper delivered to your door, and when you upgrade to an executive room, you'll get a Jacuzzi tub, 37" LCD television and a bay window or private balcony. Within a mile from many local eateries, the Wesley Inn location makes it ideal for a mid-day break and a good night's rest. The Inn's cozy fireplace rooms are a delight in the cooler months—and what's better than a warm fire to curl up next to after lots of jaunts around town with Fido? In the summer months you can enjoy the Inn's heated outdoor pool in a gated courtyard.

After a good night's rest and on a full stomach thanks to the Wesley Inn's complimentary breakfast, visit **Wilco Farm**, a farmer-owned cooperative. Wilco Farm, previously owned by Gig Harbor residents and operated under the name of Stroh's Feed Store, sits on the same piece of land upon which it was historically established. Wilco Farm is dog-friendly and well mannered, leashed dogs can join their humans while they explore the 20,000-square-foot retail store, 12,000-square-foot warehouse, and a 5,000-square-foot covered outdoor garden area. If your pup needs more active exercise, blocks from Wilco you'll find a cut-off to the paved Cushman Trail that will lead you all the way to the Narrows Bridge. All along the Cushman Trail you'll find Mutt Mitt poop dispensers thanks to Gig Harbor's **Mud Bay** outlet. With legs stretched, appetites addressed, and fresh water and treats for the road, it's time to head on out to your next location: Olympia!

OLYMPIA From Tacoma, Olympia is just 30 miles south on I-5. Besides the state capitol of Washington, Olympia is one hip town with many sites to explore. Like a lot of capital cities, many of hotels in the area are geared toward business, and honestly these do just fine when traveling with your pup, but when traveling to Olympia, we've got a little secret to share with you.

STAY For a picture perfect stay in Olympia you'll want to check out the **Hotel RL Olympia** by Red Lion. The Hotel RL is a true waterfront retreat. Situated on 12 expansive acres, it has stunning views of Capitol Lake and is engulfed in woods, offering serenity not often seen in a capital city. Hotel RL loves pups, and offers minimal pet fees and guest rooms with easy access to pet relief areas; and you'll also find free bike rentals, complimentary coffee WiFi, parking, and shuttle service, as well as a fitness center, laundry service, and an outdoor swimming pool. Hotel RL even offers a convenient Grab and Go menu, making picnic time with your pup within easy reach on the hotel's well manicured lawn. When we stay at Hotel RL, we always order avocado toast topped with salmon and a boiled egg on the side for the pup before heading out for a walk around the grounds.

p: A group of girls take a break from their prooject at AR Workshop to en-
y some attention from shop dog Russell. Above: Delicious smelling candles
d beautiful scarves are just a few of the items you will find at Tinkled Pink.

If you prefer a more urban environment, then make haste to downtown Olympia with your pup for a little retail therapy.

Belleza Ropa Clothing and Shoes is a wonderful shop where you can test your taste for wearing funky and fun outfits. There is also a little outdoor table where you can sip some coffee and rest for a spell before you move on.

SIT If all of this activity has you a tad thirsty, then you'll want to check out these pup-friendly beer places. **Northwest Beerwerks** is more than a taproom for beer, wine and cider enthusiasts. Snuggled waterside, Beerwerks offers tasty Pacific Northwest drinks that you can enjoy while your pup watches the seagulls come and go. If you get hungry, check out the street side eatery, **boKa Island Fusion**, a Hawaiian-themed food truck.

AY After a walk, it's time to hit the road and check out some of ympia's must-see sites, in particular, the **Capitol Campus**. With so uch to see, the campus offers a little bit of something for everyone. ere are six parks on the campus—the Capitol Lake, Centennial Park, eritage Park, Marathon Park, Interpretive Center, and Sylvester Park, th acres upon acres for you and your pooch to explore. We particu- ly like Heritage Park, a 24-acre park within a hop, skip and a jump Capitol Lake and downtown Olympia. Paths surround the park and pitol Lake, connecting to a number of other walking paths.

If your preference is waterfront then head to **Percival Landing**. cated on the most southern part of Puget Sound, this glorious terfront park is a gathering place for locals and visitors alike, with a o-mile walkway, picnic areas, views of the moored boats, and hands- public art features.

Another option is the **Olympia Woodland Trail**, a five-mile, relatively t, round trip trail, with over 12,000 native plants to explore.

You might also want to try **Cascadia Brewing Company** to quench your thirst. Cascadia has locally made cider, kombucha, as well as nitro, IPA, porter, red, and blonde beer. If you are interested in learning how to brew at home, Cascadia has the supplies and knowledge that will help you out.

Olympia is home to a lot of small, unique spots with outdoor seating where dogs are welcome. We've discovered a few that truly stand out for

Photo by Holly Cook

Above: AR Workshop's shop dog Russell relaxes after a busy day of entertaining guests in the art studio.

not only being dog-friendly, but also serve amazingly tasty food. **Vic's Pizzeria Wildwood** on the westside of Olympia, makes pizza, including vegan and gluten-free options, using only the freshest ingredients, and offers Pacific Northwest beer flights. Our favorite Vic's pie is the 18-inch Sherman, made with a spinach walnut pesto, topped with roasted chicken and garlic, feta and mozzarella cheese.

Feeling more like pub food? **Fish Tale Brew Pub** serves up salads and soup, small and big plate foods, as well as burgers, nachos and of course, beer. Our favorite grub from the pub is shrimp and grits, with gulf shrimp, Andouille, sofrito, and topped with sharp cheddar cheese; and ending your meal with Bourbon Pecan Pie always makes us happy.

Another one of our favorites is **Three Magnets Brew Pub**, where we always start a meal with their freshly squeezed Fizzy Lavender Lemonade. Three Magnets' menu is casual highbrow serving a seafood artisan board that offers rockfish ceviche, yearling oysters, gravlax, and crispy veggies with crackers. Three Magnets also specializes in vegetarian and vegan delicacies, including a Marinated Seitan Sandwich served on ciabatta with cilantro lime slaw and house ginger mustard BBQ sauce. Three Magnets' clam linguini is truly worth the drive to Olympia!

A good way to end the day is taking your dog for a good, long walk to burn off dinner. For this the grounds of Hotel RL come in very handy. You and your pup can wander around the 12-acres of the hotel, explore the greenery and watch the sunset sink into the Olympic mountain range. After you've stretched your legs, if you still feel like exploring you can don your swimsuit and head out to the seasonal outdoor pool, or head

to the hotel's Living Stage to take in a musical or spoken word performance. If a warm, bubbly soak is more to your liking, then sink into your hotel room's large tub and feel your muscles melt.

PLAY After a good night's sleep, and a little coffee and snack, it's time to head out with Fido for some serious play time. Don't forget a little something to munch on for your pup. There are a number of places for you to pick up a treat for your pooch. **The Pet Works** has innovative products and holistic pet treats and foods that your pup will love.

Olympia is also home to **Evergreen State College**, one of the most naturally beautiful colleges offering mile upon miles of hiking trails amidst it' 1,000 acres of forest land. Depending on where you hike at Evergreen, trai will have you traversing surprisingl thick and unspoiled woodlands whi you wander past the college's organ farm. Out favorite hike has you parking in the college's F Lot, near the corner of Driftwood and Overhulse Roads, and heading out one of the forest trails down towards the Puge Sound. As you hike out to the water of the Eld Inlet, follow the shore trai where you can beachcomb along the shore, or sit and watch for wildlife. I you and your pup are up for it, rent a kayak from the college's recreation center. The Eld Inlet shore is even interesting at night, when you can se small bioluminescent algae glowing the water.

In the south Puget Sound there ar many options for you and your pup with a whole host of dog-friendly, outdoor cafés, glorious sights to see, beaches to explore, and hiking paths to wander with your pup. 🐾

Photo by Jamie Pflughoeft

ORE INFORMATION

st Western Wesley Inn & Suites
75 Kimball Drive, Gig Harbor
3.858.9690; wesleyinn.com

tary Bark Park
100 Bujacich Rd NW, Gig Harbor
nmetparks.org

urmet Burger Shop
20 Harborview Drive, Gig Harbor
3.858.5205; facebook.com/
urmetBurgerShop

cky Dog Outfitters
04 Judson Street, Gig Harbor
3.858.6964; facebook.com/
ckyDogOutfittersGH

ckled Pink
26 Harborview Drive, Gig Harbor
3.858.1751; facebook.com/
ckledPinkGigHarbor

eritage Distilling
07 57th St Ct NW, Gig Harbor
3.509.0008; heritagedistilling.com

va & Clay Café
10 Harborview Drive, Gig Harbor
3.851.3277; javaclaycafe.com

Green Cottage Pets
3028 Harborview Drive, Gig Harbor
253.851-8806; greencottagepets.com

Gig Harbor Strength & Fitness
5775 Soundview Drive, Ste 101C
Gig Harbor; 253.432.4971
ghstrengthandfitness.com

Hotel RL Olympia
2300 Evergreen Park Dr SW
360.943.4000; redlion.com/hotel-rl/
wa/olympia/hotel-rl-olympia

Percival Landing
217 Thurston Ave NW, Olympia

Karen Fraser Woodland Trail
1600 Eastside Street SE, Olympia

Evergreen State College,
2700 Evergreen Pkwy NW, Olympia

Washington State Capitol Campus
416 Sid Snyder Ave SW, Olympia

Belleza Ropa Clothing and Shoes
101 Capitol Way N, Olympia
360.352.7672; bellezaropa.com

Northwest Beerwerks
420 Steele St SE, Olympia
northwestbeerwerks.com

Boka Island Fusion
2504 Pacific Ave SE, Olympia

Cascadia Brewing Company
211 4th Ave E, Olympia
360.943.2337; facebook.com/pg/
cascadiahomebrew

Vic's Pizzeria Wildwood
2822 Capitol Blvd SE, Olympia
360.688.1234; vicspizzaoly.com

Fish Tale Brew Pub
515 Jefferson St SE, Olympia
360.943.3650; fishbrewing.com/
fish-tale-brewpub

Three Magnets Brew Pub
600 Franklin St SE #105, Olympia
threemagnetsbrewing.com

The Pet Works
407 4th Ave E, Olympia
360.489.0134; thepetworks.net

Woodinville Wine Country

Nestled in the beautiful Sammamish River Valley, Woodinville Wine Country is home to over 100 wineries—we dug up the dog-friendly ones.

hoto by Amelia Soper

At Willows Lodge, we love pets.

Thanks to our WVIP (Willows Very Important Pet) Program, amenities for our four-legged friends include a doggie room service menu, map and directions for pet and owner walks and Willows Lodge water. In addition, your dog will receive a welcome card, a recent issue of Citydog Magazine and a doggie bed with turndown service including a night-time doggie biscuit. (Warning: your dog may never want to leave.)

Walk to local dog-friendly tasting rooms

14580 NE 145th Street
Woodinville, WA 98072
willowslodge.com | **425.424.3900**
$75 pet fee per stay.

WHETHER YOU VISIT THE HOLLYWOOD DISTRICT OR WAREHOUSE DISTRICT, THE WEST VALLEY DISTRICT OR DOWNTOWN DISTRICT, DOGS ARE WELCOME AT MANY OF THE TASTING ROOMS IN THE WOODINVILLE WINE COUNTRY REGION.

Originally, Woodinville was home to the Sammamish natives and through time became the more populated suburban hamlet it is today, home to numerous wineries, cideries, and breweries, and is the gateway to a lot of outdoor fun such as bicycle riding, river kayaking, and hot air ballooning. In 1969 Woodinville hosted the Seattle Pop Festival at Gold Creek Park and people came from miles around to hear The Doors, Led Zeppelin, Chuck Berry, The Guess Who, Bo Diddley, and Alice Cooper just to name a few of the illustrious musical acts. Maybe that's why the wine housed in the Woodinville area is so rocking delicious!

The downtown area of Woodinville has a bustling farmers market on Saturdays from May through September. You can visit award-winning Molbak's Garden+Home and be be amazed at all of the unique and abundant selections of plants, flowers, trees, pots, and lawn furniture. If you enjoy bicycle riding, bring your equipment including your dog's bicycle carrier so that you can tour the 11-mile paved Sammamish River Trail.

There are numerous pooch-loving places to eat, including Purple Cafe, Dirty Bucket Brewing Company, Teddy's Bigger Burgers, and Viva Pizzeria.

With its location so close to Seattle, Woodinville makes for a great day trip with Fido. Or, if you want to make a staycation out of your visit, don't worry, we've dug up one of the pup-friendliest, most luxurious accommodations in the region, **Willows Lodge**.

Above from left: Thya and the Spirit of Haida Gwaii, one of two bronze sculptures by North Coast Native artist Bill Reid; strawberries grow in the Lodge's environmentally sustainable garden.

Photos by Amelia Soper

Woodinville

WITH SO MANY DOG-FRIENDLY WINERIES, A VISIT TO WOODINVILLE IS A MUST FOR WINE LOVERS AND DOG LOVERS ALIKE.

The Woodinville area is home to over 100 tasting rooms, many that welcome dogs, so bringing your four-legged friend is a must, especially when you stay at **Willows Lodge**, a dog-friendly, luxury resort spread over five landscaped acres bordering the Sammamish River, and located in the heart of Woodinville's wine tasting circuit.

STAY When you make reservations at Willows Lodge, be sure to let them know you will be joined by your canine companion. Upon arrival, you will be greeted by the friendly staff who fawn over your pup like the VIP he or she is, and the pampering will continue once in your spacious, rustic-chic room.

Willows Lodge offers a Very Important Pet Program that features amenities for your four-legged friend, including a doggie room service menu, walking map and directions for pets and their owners and bottled water because tap water just won't do for your VIP. What's truly special is the welcome card addressed specifically to your pup along with a few treats and a fleece doggie bed complete with turn down service and the most recent issue of CityDog Magazine.

Simply put, Willows Lodge knows how to cater to you and your pup. Each year, they see about 600 canine

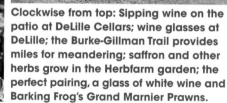

Clockwise from top: Sipping wine on the patio at DeLille Cellars; wine glasses at DeLille; the Burke-Gillman Trail provides miles for meandering; saffron and other herbs grow in the Herbfarm garden; the perfect pairing, a glass of white wine and Barking Frog's Grand Marnier Prawns.

Photos by Amelia Soper

GETTING HERE Follow I-405 North. Take exit 20B: NE 124th St, and turn right onto NE 124th St. Left at 132nd Ave NE. Right at NE 143rd Place. Proceed down hill and over railroad tracks. Stay right onto NE 145th St. Willows Lodge will be on your left.

Photos by Amelia Soper

bove: The grassy area adjacent to the fireside patio at Willows dge is the perfect place to relax. Right: Art is everywhere; this one structure is home to a bronze sculpture of a killer whale spirit.

uests at their property, a testament to how dog friendly they truly are. dog friendly in fact, they have a special room service menu just for gs that includes yummy items like Hungry Mongrel Steak, broiled ef strips with brown rice and carrots. Or, Chick, Chick, Chicken, a vely combination of chicken loaf, broccoli and carrots. Just pick up the none in your room, push the numbers for room service, and place your rder. Make sure to let the chef know just how Fido likes his steak, rare, edium, or well done!

Willows Lodge also has fabulous amenities included for their two-gged guests. In addition to two queen sized beds with down duvets nd Italian linens, there is a stone hearth with gas fireplace, comfy ating area, and a spa tub with separate walk-in shower—both aturing London's Moulton & Brown bath goodies. There is also a very rge flat screen HDTV, complimentary wireless Internet access, fully ocked refrigerator with snacks and beverages for purchase, Keurig offee-maker, as well as a selection of herbal and black teas, plus terry oth robes and spa slippers. Pure luxury.

All of the lodge's 14 dog-friendly rooms are located on the ground floor, ith a garden patio and sliding door for easy access to the outdoors, where network of trails for exploring awaits. And, there is much to explore. Grab ome of the Willows's bottled water, leash up your VIP, and follow the trail outh along the Sammamish River and you will find the lovely Herbfarm arden, home to potbellied pigs Borage and Basil, who are seemingly nfazed by dog's walking by. Further exploration of the gardens reveals a ounty of herbs and edible plants that will eventually be used in dishes at

the world renowned **Herbfarm Restaurant**, located on the property.

PLAY Heading north along the lodge's trail system reveals even more hidden, artistic treasures. A small stone building that looks like it could be out of the set of Lord of the Rings houses a bronze sculpture of a killer whale's spirit. Further north you'll find the Spirit of Haida Gwaii, two large bronze heads cast from the original work of Haida artist Bill Reid. Also nearby is the Fireside Garden, where you can take a break from our wanderings to enjoy a glass of wine. While dogs are not allowed on the fireside patio, simply relax in one of Adirondack chairs on the adjacent grassy area, where dogs are warmly welcomed. Tip: Ask for a water bowl for your four-legged friend.

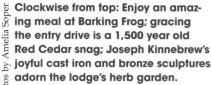

Photos by Amelia Soper

Clockwise from top: Enjoy an amazing meal at Barking Frog; gracing the entry drive is a 1,500 year old Red Cedar snag; Joseph Kinnebrew's joyful cast iron and bronze sculptures adorn the lodge's herb garden.

SIT Willows Lodge is built for relaxing and conversation. Take your time, enjoy meeting visitors and sharing stories about the wineries in the area that you have planned to visit tomorrow. When the proverbial dinner bell rings, it's time to enjoy one of our favorite restaurants, the **Barking Frog**. The warm and bistro-like restaurant embraces the same rustic and refined feel of the lodge and the menu embodies all that is marvelous about the Pacific Northwest. We recommend starting with oysters on the half shell with a champagne mignonette, or the Penn Cove mussels in a coconut-curry broth—followed by the beet salad, with endive, arugula, pistachio, confit orange syrup and warm goat cheese puree. For the main course it's a toss up between the scallops, with quinoa, cherry tomatoes, cucumber, avocado-

tomatillo salsa, spiced mango and candied jalapeno, or the ribeye, with hand cut fries, aioli, thyme butter and veal demi glace. As you enjoy your meal, feel free to ask for wine recommendations that will complement the flavors. One of our favorites is a bottle of Woodinville's own Efeste Final Final. Dessert is a must, and selections include key lime pie with speculoos crust, coconut cucumber sorbet, ginger kaffir lime snow and blackberry margarita coulis, and the crème brûlée du jour. Yes, you will need a walk after dinner and luckily your pup will need one also, so lace up your tennis shoes and take in the cool air as you walk among the lodge's lovely grounds together.

PLAY The following morning, while you wait for the wineries to open check out the **Burke-Gilman Trail**. Perfect for a walk or jog, this scenic 26-mile trail borders the lodge and runs all the way to Seattle. It's perfect for walking with your pooch, just keep an eye out for bikers and rollerbladers. The Sammamish River Trail segment of the Burke-Gilman Trail, which is next to Willows Lodge, parallels the Sammamish River for nearly 11 miles. If you're feeling particularly ambitious, you can take this walk that ends at **Marymoor Park**, home to a 48-acre off-leash dog park. If you brought your bicycle with you, you can make it a leisurely ride with your dog in tow and have a fun morning where you sip coffee while your dog plays in the park.

Working out your dog's energy is a good idea as you head out

Above: The 14 pet-friendly rooms are located on the ground floor, with a garden patio and sliding glass door for easy access.

or a day of wine tasting. It's also a good idea to know which wineries offer food for tasting, and then bring additional items that you and your dog might want to nosh on throughout the trip. Extra water is always welcome, and make sure to refill your poop bag holder as necessary. After a luxurious soak in your tub, and a quick brush of your pup's fur, both of you are ready to head out to your first winery. Before you head out, be sure to pick up a walking map at the front desk, featuring nearby wineries, breweries and distilleries.

First, we recommend the tasting room at the nearby **DeLille Cellars Carriage House**. Head to the gorgeous and dog-friendly outdoor patio and try the Doyenne rosé. Doyenne means "a woman who is the most respected or prominent person in a particular field." Delicious, the Columbia Valley rosé smells and tastes of watermelon, strawberries, cherries, cantaloupe, with a hint of basil. Pure summer! We also recommend the D2, a delightful blend of merlot, cabernet sauvignon, cabernet Franc and petit verdot. DeLille Cellars' tasting flight features four wines, that change based on availability, and costs $20 or $25. The tasting fee is waived if you purchase two or more bottles of wine.

Located right next door is **Brian Carter Cellars**, where you and your pooch are invited to enjoy their "little yellow tasting room," where they practice the art of blending. Brian Carter Cellars has a patio and a deck area that creates a perfect place to sample wines and sit back to take in the flavors. Savor the sip of Oriana. Latin for "golden lady," Oriana is a very rich smelling wine with hints of apricot, orange, pear, apple and honey, and ends with a delightful crispness that combines the fruity flavors. Another wine to sip, if you are a Grenache lover, is their Byzance with ripe black

cherry and earthy, herbal notes. But, you really can't go wrong—all of Brian Carter Cellars' wines are truly inspired and the dog-friendly atmosphere makes it all the better.

Last in our selection has you returning back towards Willows Lodge. **Fidélitas Red Mountain** tasting room has been open since 2013 and in that short amount of time, has built a reputation for quality. Fidélitas offers daily tasting with $15 wine flights, or free with purchase. Try the Semillon, with notes of honeysuckle and pear, mixed with pink grapefruit and papaya. Another wine to try is their Optu Red Mountain, a blend of cabernet sauvignon, merlot, petit verdot and cabernet Franc—its flavor profile is a mix of tobacco and black cherry and is perfect for an evening of good conversation spent with the people and pups you cherish.

However, your adventure doesn't have to end here. We've compiled a list of more Fido-friendly wineries starting on the following pages. 🐾

MORE INFORMATION

Willows Lodge
14580 NE 145th Street, Woodinville
425.424.3900; willowslodge.com

DeLille Cellars
14421 Woodinville Redmond Rd NE
425.877.9472; delillecellars.com

Brian Carter Cellars
14419 Woodinville-Redmond Rd NE
425.806.9463; briancartercellars.com

Fidélitas Red Mountain
14467 Redmond-Woodinville Rd NE
425.558.9001; fidelitaswines.com

Photo by Amelia Soper

WOODINVILLE WINE COUNTRY

Dogs can't drink wine, but they sure are fun to drink wine with—so we dug up some of the best, dog-friendly wineries in Woodinville and compiled them here, so you have a handy list to take with you on your next wine tasting adventure, whether it's a pinot at Patterson or full-bodied red at Brian Carter—we've got the scoop.

Brian Carter Cellars (*briancartercellars.com*)
14419 Woodinville-Redmond Rd NE, Woodinville

Brian Carter features a large deck and lawn great for picnics and wine tasting. Dogs with inside voices are also welcome in the tasting room.

Matthews Winery (*matthewswinery.com*)
16116 140th Place NE, Woodinville

Matthews Winery offers eight acres with grass, picnic tables, and places to walk your dog near the small stream and heavily treed hillside. Bring a Frisbee or tennis ball to toss with Fido! Water bowls are available upon request.

DeLille Cellars (*delillecellars.com*)
14421 Woodinville Redmond Road NE, Woodinville

The DeLille Cellars Carriage House Tasting Room offer endless doggie treats and all the water your best friend could need. Enjoy a relaxed wine tasting experience in the spacious outdoor tasting area perfect for pups.

J. Bookwalter Tasting Studio (*bookwalterwines.com*)
14810 NE 145th Street, Bldg. B, Woodinville,

J. Bookwalter loves dogs of all types and sizes at its Woodinville tasting studio. Patrons can enjoy a glass of wine with dogs on the sizeable grassy area or patio. A food truck is often available from the patio.

orthwest Cellars Winery (*northwestcellars.com*)
909 124th Avenue NE, Kirkland

et off the beaten path and where dogs are welcome in
orthwest Cellars' tasting room. The winery supports
any local animal organizations including Homeward
et, Seattle Humane Society, K-DOG, Pasado's, Old
og Haven, Purrfect Pals, AHELP and Seattle Purebred
escue with approximately $60,000 donated to local
imal charities in 2018.

tis Kenyon (*otiskenyonwine.com*)
525 148th Ave NE, Woodinville

ocated on the lower level garden that can be entered
om its parking lot, the Otis Kenyon Woodinville tast-
g room invites you to experience a hidden garden
sis. Savor wine from the Walla Walla Valley with
ur dog in tow. You will both enjoy the peaceful
mosphere.

tterson Cellars (*pattersoncellars.com*)
505 148th Avenue NE, Woodinville

tterson Cellars attracts wine tasters and their canine
mpanions with fresh water bowls, treats and a
aded patio area.

y River Meadery (*skyrivermead.com*)
270 Woodinville Redmond Rd NE, Redmond

y River Meadery welcomes well-behaved dogs.
ashed dogs are welcome in the tasting room and the
ounds include a large grassy pasture for playtime and
isbee chasing. Water available inside and out.

evens Winery (*stevenswinery.com*)
510 142nd Ave NE, Woodinville

op by the Warehouse District to sample Stevens Win-
y's six reds or two white wines with your furry friend.

illiam Church Winery (*intecellars.com*)
455 Woodinville-Redmond Rd NE, Woodinville

illiam Church makes wine tasting fun and casual,
ith limited use of new oak that makes its wines ap-
oachable. Weiner dogs to Weimaraners are welcome
this winery that faithfully donates to local shelters as
ell as rescue ventures.

MORE DOG-FRIENDLY WOODINVILLE WINERIES

- Davenport Cellars (*davenportcellars.com*)
- J & A's Winery (*jandaswinery.com*)
- Red Sky Winery (*redskywinery.com*)
- Page Cellars (*pagecellars.com*)
- Guardian Cellars (*guardiancellers.com*)
- Covington Cellars (*covingtoncellars.com*)
- Two Vintners (*twovintners.com*)
- Armstrong Family Winery (*armstrongwinery.com*)
- Piccola Cellars (*facebook.com/PiccolaCellars*)
- Genoa Cellars (*genoacellars.com*)
- Callahan Cellars (*callahancellars.com*)
- Vessel Wines (*vesselwines.com*)
- William Church (*tintecellars.com*)
- Cuillin Hills (*tintecellars.com*)
- Barrage Cellars (*barragecellars.com*)
- Darby Cellars (*darbywinery.com*)
- Forgeron (*forgeroncellars.com*)
- Soft Tail Distiller (*softtailspirits.com*)
- Patit Creek (*facebook.com/pages/Patit-Creek-Cellars*)
- Pleasant Hills (*pleasanthillcellars.com*)
- Belmonte Cellars (*facebook.com/BelmonteCellarsWine*)
- Icon Cellars (*iconcellars.com*)
- Fidelitas (*fidelitaswines.com*)
- Sparkman (*sparkmancellars.com*)
- Mark Ryan (*markryanwinery.com*)
- Lachini (*lachinivinyards.com*)
- Zerba (*zerbacellars.com*)
- Top of the Barrel (*facebook.com/pages/Top-of-the-Barrel*)
- Lauren Ashton (*lauraashtoncellars.com*)
- Nine Hats (*ninehatswines.com*)
- Chandler Reach (*chandlerreach.com*)

San Juan Island

With 247 days of sunshine a year, and half the rain of Seattle, San Juan Island is the perfect year-round getaway for you and your pooch.

Photo by Julie Clegg

VODKA *for* DOG PEOPLE

vodkafordogpeople.com

We created Vodka for Dog People to unite with friends, fans, and partners to make the world a better place for pets and their families far and wide.

Visit vodkafordogpeople.com to get involved.

 /titosvodka

@titosvodka

 @titosvodka
@vodkafordogpeople

GF Gluten-Free **TitosVodka.com ★ Crafted to be savored responsibly.** DISTILLED & BOTTLED BY FIFTH GENERATION INC. 40% ALC./VOL. © 2017 TITO'S HANDMADE VODKA.

BRING A CAMERA, COMFORTABLE WALKING SHOES AND YOUR CANINE, BUT LEAVE YOUR CARES BEHIND. THE SERENITY OF SAN JUAN ISLAND BECKONS.

ust one square mile in size, Friday Harbor is the very walkable ub of San Juan Island. The most populated of the islands, San Juan is me to art galleries, museums, bookstores and antique shops. Sample a uquet of boutiques, stop for a café lunch or enjoy a fresh seafood din- r overlooking the harbor. With a wide array of dining options, we're re you'll find a new favorite each time you visit. Spend an afternoon The Whale Museum to learn about our unique ecosystem, or brush on island history at the San Juan Historical Society & Museum. For orld-class art, visit the San Juan Islands Museum of Art (SJIMA) or the n Juan Community Theatre.

Friday Harbor is also home to a large marina. Spend time walking e docks, buying fresh seafood, or looking for Popeye the harbor seal. om the marina, you can take a number of tours and trips. Hop in a ayak or go out on a whale and wildlife watching tour to see the spec- cular creatures that call the islands home. If you're looking for more utdoor adventures, spend the day hiking or biking through the island's any trails and scenic routes. And of course, after a day of adventure, eat yourself to a meal at one of the many restaurants on San Juan Is-

land. Consider fine dining at McMillin's in Roche Harbor, fresh island cuisine at Duck Soup, or a meal with a view at Friday Harbor House.

When you are ready to venture out of Friday Harbor, the Scenic Byway routes (North, South and West) take you through rolling farmlands, along stunning coastlines, and past some of the main attractions on San Juan Island, such as Cattle Point Lighthouse, Ameri- can Camp, Lime Kiln Point Lighthouse, English Camp, San Juan Vineyards and more. Follow the signs for a truly beautiful adventure!

Above: It's a tranquil setting at San Juan Island's Lakedale Resort.

Photo by Julie Clegg

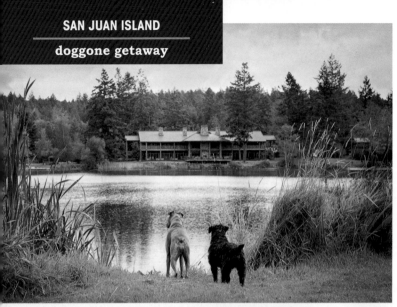

San Juan Island

LAKEDALE RESORT ON SAN JUAN ISLAND OFFERS YOU AND ROVER A TRANQUIL RETREAT.

Just a scenic ferry ride or a shor flight from Seattle lies a paradise for the adventurous spirit: San Juan Island. Whether you yearn for the slow pace of island time or the excitement of new experiences this Washington gem delivers— especially for dog lovers.

STAY One such dog-friendly oasis is **Lakedale Resort**. Surrounded b three freshwater lakes on 82 acres, Lakedale is nestled between Roche Harbor and Friday Harbor.

Lakedale Resort offers guests a choice between five types of accommodations: the romantic Lodge, an elegant, four bedroom Lake House, custom-built Canvas Cabins, individual campsites and family-friendly log cabins. Only th log cabins and campsites are dog friendly and we recommend optin for one of the cozy log cabins.

There are just six cabins in all, each featuring two bedrooms, two full baths, dining nook, fireplace and large cedar deck. Other amenities include a kitchen with microwave, full-size oven with range, refrigerator, TV and DVD player (guests can borrow DVDs from the main Lodge). Each cabin also features complimentary breakfast fixings that include scone and pancake mix, granola, milk, orange juice, butter and syrup. Located outside each cabin, there is

Clockwise from top: Scout and Ziggy enjoy the scenery at Lakedale Resort; the Meadow sits adjacent to cabin six at Lakedale Resort and is a great place for dogs to run; bundles of lavender at Pelindaba Lavender Farm; "Entry" by Tom Small is one of many pieces of art at San Juan Island's Sculpture Park.

fire pit with a grill for cooking and a picnic table.

As mentioned, the resort is surrounded by 82 scenic acres, providing guests with a range of outdoor activities including hiking on the many trails and paths, playing horseshoes, barbecuing and bike riding. There are three freshwater lakes for swimming as well as paddle boats, row boats and canoes to rent. Or guests are welcome to try their hand at trout fishing in the stocked lakes (permit required). If you are at Lakedale in the off-season, it can seem like you have the entire place to yourself, but in peak season, the place is bustling with activity.

PLAY Even with all there is to see and do at Lakedale Resort,

Photo by Julie Clegg

SAN JUAN ISLAND

doggone getaway

Scout scopes out the prairies at American Camp National Historical Park.

visit to San Juan Island merits some serious exploration, so load up the dogs and hit the road. Your first stop is the **Sculpture Park**, located within walking distance to Roche Harbor on Westcott Bay. The 20-acre park features more than 100 pieces of incredible art including works in bronze, stone, wood, metal, glass and ceramic by noted artists from the Pacific Northwest; Georgia Gerber for one, known for her Pike Place Market bronze sculpted pig. For art- and dog-lovers alike, the Sculpture Park is a must-see on your island adventure. For a virtual tour, visit sjima.org.

After exploring the Sculpture Park, drive the short distance to **Roche Harbor**, a lovely hamlet featuring a marina, shops and three waterfront restaurants. At Roche, take a stroll around the marina and grab some nibbles at the historic **Company Store** grocery (where you can donate your change to the Friday Harbor Animal Shelter for pups less fortunate). On the way back, take Roche Harbor Rd, grab a view of Sportsman Lake, and stop at the **San Juan Winery** for a tasting or two. While you're there, grab some Buddy's Biscuits for your biscuit loving buddy.

The next stop on your journey is **English Camp**, but first, a bit of history. On June 15, 1859, an American farmer shot and killed a Hudson's Bay Company pig rooting in his potato patch. By doing so, he nearly started a war between the United States and Great Britain. Over the next 12 years, the two countries jointly occupied San Juan Island with their own camps on opposite ends of the island until the dispute was settled, ending the so-called war in which the only casualty was a pig.

The American and British camps are now designated national historical parks, with English Camp situated on the north end of San Juan Island on Garrison Bay. The setting is beautiful with trails meandering through as well as an open grassy area at water's edge. A highlight of the expansive park is the formal garden, originally a vegetable garden planted in 1867 to feed the troops. The garden today was planted in 1972 to commemorate the 100th anniversary of the boundary settlement, and features 13 beds of flowers and shrubs planted in a circular pattern in the tradition of formal English gardens.

Next, hit the road again, this time in search of **Krystal Acres Alpaca Farm**. While Krystal Acres is not dog friendly, for animal lovers it is still worth a visit. The farm sits on 80

Photos by Julie Clegg

Clockwise from top: The lighthouse at Lime Kiln Point State Park; Lakedale offers boating and canoeing; Houdini the alpaca at Krystal Acres.

on-site distillery where the essential oils are extracted from the flowers to create a wide range of botanical, culinary, therapeutic, household and pet care products.

If you are curious about the pet care products, lavender is highly effective in repelling insects plus its soothing, antiseptic and anesthetic properties help with sensitive skin. Grab a bottle of lavender pet shampoo and some gourmet lavender chicken treats in the gift shop before heading out to your next destination.

As those of us who live in the Pacific Northwest know, the San Juan Islands are prime whale watching waters and **Lime Kiln Point State Park** is an ideal overlook to keep an eye out for these amazing creatures.

With 2,550 feet of waterfront, Lime Kiln Point is considered one of the best places in the world to view whales from land, with peak whale-watching months from May through September. With fingers crossed, hang out at the overlook for a whale sighting while taking in the breathtaking scenery.

Even at the height of the summer season, you can find solitude and experience nature on San Juan Island, especially at your next

acres, with an ever-growing herd of more than 50 alpacas. Stroll around the farm, pet an alpaca or two then browse through the extraordinary selection of super-soft alpaca sweaters, coats, yarn and cuddly alpaca toys in the Country Store.

Returning to the car where your dog anxiously awaits, head next to the **Pelindaba Lavender Farm**. It's a short distance from Krystal Acres, and more importantly, this farm is dog friendly, for the most part. Dogs can wander the grounds with you, they just can't be in the organically-certified lavender fields, where Pelindaba cultivates the flowers. However, there is plenty to explore with your pooch including the

Relax with your pups on the spacious deck at Lakedale Resort's cabin six.

o, the **American Camp
tional Historical Park**.
ether you're on the
iries, rocky hilltops,
p forest or saltwater
oreline, there is plenty to
olore with your pooch.
e vast, open prairie is
iquely beautiful and
her unexpected in the
stern portion of the
cific Northwest, where
ergreen forests dominate
e landscape. Here you
n stroll through the
ne wildflowers and
sses as native peoples
oerienced hundreds of
rs ago. American Camp
o features an expansive
ich to explore with your
ir-legged friend as well
enjoy a game of fetch.

As the day comes
a close and tummies
gin to grumble, head to
iday Harbor for a bite to
. Friday Harbor might
small in population
2,260, but it's big on
ırm. This quaint seaside
mlet boasts a multitude
restaurants offering
e finest in dining, from
rely open-air bistros to
licious ice cream parlors.
e recommend the
sk & Schooner Public
ouse & Restaurant, with
ingeness crab macaroni
d cheese on the menu
iong other things. After
ur meal, take a stroll
ough Friday Harbor
iere you will find shops

galore, offering everything from clothing and jewelry to paintings and sculptures—all hand-crafted by local artists. Most of the shops are dog friendly, particularly **Browne's Home Center**, where your pooch will be warmly welcomed with treats. Up the street a bit, pay a visit to the newly-opened **Eddie & Friends** dog park where your Rover can run free. It also includes a separate small dog area. To finish the day, be sure to score some mint chocolate chip at the famous ice cream stand near the ferry dock. 🐾

Photo by Julie Clegg

MORE INFORMATION

Lakedale Resort
4313 Roche Harbor Road
Friday Harbor, Wash.
360.378.2350; lakedale.com

Sculpture Park
9083 Roche Harbor Rd, Friday Harbor

Roche Harbor Marina
248 Reuben Memorial Dr, Friday Harbor
360.378.2155; rocheharbor.com

San Juan Vineyard
3136 Roche Harbor Rd, Friday Harbor
360.378.9463; sanjuanvineyard.com

English Camp
4668 Cattle Point Road, Friday Harbor

American Camp
4668 Cattle Point Rd, Friday Harbor

Krystal Acres Alpaca Farm
3501 W Valley Rd, Friday Harbor
360.378.6125; krystalacres.com

Pelindaba Lavender Farm
45 Hawthorne Ln, Friday Harbor
360.378.4248; pelindabalavender.com

Lime Kiln Point State Park
1567 West Side Rd, Friday Harbor

Cask & Schooner Public House
1 Front St, Friday Harbor
360.378.2922; caskandschooner.com

Browne's Home Center
860 Mullis St, Friday Harbor
360.378.2168; browneshomecenter.com

Eddie & Friends Dog Park
Mullis Street, Friday Harbor

North Central Cascades

Considered Washington's playground, this region offers up a whole lot of fun for you and Fido, from Nordic skiing to wine tasting to cooling off in a crystal clear lake.

Photo by Julie Austin

A TREAT FOR HIM.

A RETREAT FOR YOU.

The gorgeous scenery and many outdoor adventures at Sleeping Lady Resort are sure to bring a smile to your face, and your dog won't be able to stop wagging his tail! While our luxurious spa and fine cuisine are for humans only, our Canine Companion Room is set up to pamper your pet – with cozy doggie beds, water and food bowls, and complimentary treats. And Roki, our resident Icelandic Shepherd, loves sharing his huge outdoor playground with all furry friends.

Certified
Ⓑ
Corporation

**Book your Canine Companion
Room today at SleepingLady.com
or call 800.574.2123.**

SLEEPING LADY
A MOUNTAIN RESORT

WASHINGTON HAS EVERYTHING A NATURE LOVER (AND DOG LOVER) COULD WANT: SNOWCAPPED MOUNTAINS, OCEAN BEACHES, THICK RAINFORESTS, UNINHABITED ISLANDS—AND THE NORTH CENTRAL REGION OF THE STATE IS NO EXCEPTION.

Nestled in the Cascade Mountains is Leavenworth, your gateway to all things adventure. With more to offer than just brats and beer, this Bavarian hamlet offers everything from hiking, biking, river rafting, skiing, golf and snowshoeing to wine tasting, dining, shopping, and the arts. But, if beer is your prference, you can quench your thirst on the outdoor patio at Icicle Brewery (it's dog friendly).

Just east of Leavenworth is **Wenatchee**, where you will find even more adventure, whether it's wine tasting or floating the Wenatchee River on a paddleboard with your pooch.

Heading north on US-97, **Lake Chelan** promises four seasons worth of fun with Fido, with 300 days of sunshine and a plethora of pooch-friendly places to sit, stay and play. Chelan is surrounded by wineries, so if you're up for some tasting, you are in the right place, but it also offers hiking, biking, boating and blueberries (yes, blueberries, but more on that later).

Looping back on Highway 20, the **Methow Valley** is a Mecca for outdoor enthusiasts and dog lovers alike and the historic town of Winthrop, located in the heart of it all, maintains its frontier spirit thanks to the town's Old West theme—wooden boardwalks, old time storefronts and small town charm—all of which is back-dropped by mountain peaks, expansive farmland, horse ranches, rolling hills and a river running through it.

With year-round activities, the valley draws visitors looking for adventure from river rafting, hiking, rock climbing and mountain biking in the summer, to cross country skiing and snow-shoeing in the winter. Just note, US-20 closes in the winter and opens back up in spring.

Scout and Ziggy enjoy a winter stroll at Sleeping Lady Mountain Resort.

Photo by Julie Clegg

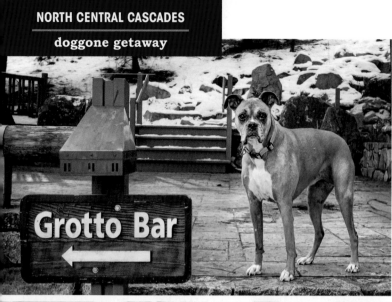

Leavenworth

LEAVE YOUR CARES BEHIND (BUT NOT YOUR CANINE) AND HEAD TO LEAVENWORTH.

Nestled in the Cascade Mountains is Leavenworth, a Bavarian hamlet with more to offer than just brats and beer. The region offers year-round adventures from hiking, biking, river rafting, skiing, golf and snowshoeing to wine tasting, dining, shopping, and the arts. And, after a this adventure, you can quench your thirst on the outdoor patio at Icicle Brewery (it's dog friendly).

There seems to be something always happening in Leavenworth no matter the season including the Christmas Lighting Festival in December, when the village is lit with hundreds of thousands of light (gorgeous). Oktoberfest in October, features live music, German food, arts and crafts, and activities for the whole family (and did we mention beer?). Throughout the summer, you can enjoy outdoor concerts plus Village Art in the Park, the longest continually running outdoor art show in the state.

STAY Pet-friendly places to stay include **Sleeping Lady Mountain Resort** and **Icicle Village Resort**. Sleeping Lady sits on 67 acres at the base of its namesake, Sleeping Lady Mountain, on the banks of Icicle Creek. The resort's Canine Companion Program in its dog-designated cabins (six total) features a cozy dog bed, water and food bowls, and complimentary treats. The cabins also feature a queen-

Clockwise from top: Scout leads the way to The Grotto at Sleeping Lady Resort; play a game of Chinese checkers in the resort's library; a wide variety of spirits are available at The Grotto; enjoy a cold one at Icicle Brewery.

GETTING HERE Travel east on I-90 past Cle Elum. Take Exit 85 towards Wenatchee. Go east on State Rt. 970 to US-97. Follow Hwy 97 north over Blewett Pass to the junction of Hwy 2. Turn left on Hwy 2 to Leavenworth.

zed bed and double-decker
unk bed, accommodating
o to four people—perfect for
milies traveling with their
rry friends.

T For happy hour, enjoy a
cktail at **The Grotto**. Serving
ine, beer and spirits, The
rotto offers a relaxing place
toast with friends or unwind
ter a day of outdoor adven-
re. For dinner, the meals
the **Kingfisher Restaurant
nd Wine Bar** are chef's choice
nd served buffet style in the
dge-like setting. All items
e prepared with organic and
cally sourced ingredients,
any from the resort's own
vo-acre organic garden.

TAY At the super dog-friendly
icle Village Resort**, they treat your pooch like part of the family, which he
, of course! Fido will feel right at home in one of the resort's 26 pet-friendly
oms. Upon check-in, he'll receive his own doggy bag and once settled into
e room, the resort has a variety of amenities for you to enjoy, including a
mplimentary breakfast buffet at **J.J. Hills Fresh Grill**. The restaurant is
so open for happy hour and dinner and the oudoor patio features views of
e mountains. You can also pamper yourself at the resort's Alpine Spa plus
ere are plenty of options for play including a video arcade, miniature golf,
orts court, two swimming pools with Jacuzzi, and much more.

T The cute Bavarian-themed downtown section of Leavenworth is only
mile walk from Icicle Resort and a perfect distance for working up an
ppetite to eat at one of the many dog-friendly restaurants. Choose between
rabbing a burger and sneaking your dog some fries at **Fresh Burger Café**,
pping chunks of bread in the legendary fondue from **Uncle Uli's Pub**,
njoying a classic German brat at the **Munchen Haus**, or grabbing a slice at
e **Leavenworth Pizza Company**.

After dinner, if beer is your libation of choice, head over to **Icicle Brewing
ompany**. You'll know you're there by the smell of warm hops wafting out
f the taproom. Across the street you can lounge on an outdoor loveseat and
p wine at **Icicle Ridge Winery** or enjoy a few sips indoors at one of our
vorites, **Goose Ridge Estate** tasting room.

LAY If your agenda includes adventure, the perfect place to escape the
eat with your pooch is on the water. Float the Wenatchee River in an
ner-tube with **Blue Sky Outfitters**, take your own stand-up-paddleboard

(SUP)—or rent one from **Osprey Rafting Company**—and head to Lake Wenatchee, Fish Lake or Confluence State Park to SUP with your pup.

At **Cove Resort** at Fish Lake, you can also rent pontoon boats for a more leisurely time on the water. The resort has life jackets for people, but if you forgot one for your pooch, swing by **A Paw Above** in Leavenworth, where you will find doggie life jackets and pretty much everything else you need for your adventures in the area.

STAY In nearby Wenatchee (east on US-2, then south on WA-285), more adventure awaits and the pooch-friendly place to stay is **The Coast Hotel**. It's right in the center of the historic downtown area and within walking distance to an array of

Above: SUP with the pups at Fish Lake. Next page: Enjoy a bottle of wine at Goose Ridge Estate's dog friendly tasting room.

Photo by Julie Austin

Photo by Julie Austin

entertainment and shopping as well as riverfront activities. They even welcome doggie guests with a goody bag and humans with a list of dog-friendly wineries in the region.

PLAY A short walk across a bridge from the hotel takes you to the **Pybus Public Market**, a year-round farmers market with local shops. Enjoy a fresh modern Latin dinner on the patio at **SOUTH** or a beer at the **Wenatchee Valley Brewing Company**. Walk off all that food and drink along the nearby **Apple Capital Loop Trail**. It's an 11-mile paved multi-use loop trail along the river that crosses the Columbia at the north and south ends. If you are a night owl, the trail is lighted until midnight on the west side for an evening stroll.

If it's a weekend between 10 a.m. and 4 p.m., you can "park" your dog at **Club Pet** for $5 an hour while you explore the rest of the market for an hour or two. Don't feel bad for leaving Fido out of the fun because you're helping other animals. Club Pet is operated by the Wenatchee Valley Humane Society and all of the proceeds go to support homeless animals.

In the morning, head down the street to **Café Mela** for coffee roasted in-house. If your day includes wine tasting, start at **Stemilt Creek Winery** a few blocks away. You also don't want to miss **Chateau Faire LePont**. You'll be hard pressed to find a more dog-friendly winery. They have two winery dogs, a fenced off-leash area with a beautiful garden, and a Yappy Hour every Friday night in the summer. 🐾

MORE INFORMATION

Sleeping Lady Mountain Resort
7375 Icicle Road, Leavenworth,
800.574.2123; sleepinglady.com

Icicle Village Resort
505 Highway 2, Leavenworth
800.961.0162; iciclevillage.com

Fresh Burger Café
923 Commercial Street, Leavenworth
509.548.3300; freshburgercafe.com

Icicle Brewing Company
935 Front Street, Leavenworth
509.548.2739; iciclebrewing.com

Apple Capital Loop Trail
E 5th St. and N. Worthen Street

Icicle Ridge Winery
920 Front Street, Leavenworth
509.470.8738; icicleridgewinery.com

Goose Ridge Estate Tasting Room
920 Front Street, Leavenworth
509.470.8676; gooseridge.com

Blue Sky Outfitters
800.228.7238; blueskyoutfitters.com

The Cove Resort
22494 Chiwawa Loop Road
Leavenworth; 509.763.3130
coveresortatfishlake.com

Osprey Rafting Company
Icicle Rd & Hwy 2, Leavenworth
509.548.6800; ospreyrafting.com

A Paw Above
900 Front Suite M, Leavenworth
509.548.3647; leavenworthpetstore.co

The Coast Hotel
201 North Wenatchee Avenue
Wenatchee; 509.662.1234
coasthotels.com

Pybus Public Market
3 N Worthen St, Wenatchee
509.888.3900; pybuspublicmarket.or

SOUTH
3 N Worthen St, Wenatchee
509.888.5463; southrestaurants.com

Wenatchee Valley Brewing Co.
3 N Worthen Street, Wenatchee
wenatcheevalleybrewing.com

Club Pet Lodging & Day Camp
3 N Worthen Street, Wenatchee
509.888.7387; wenatcheehumane.org

Café Mela
17 N Wenatchee Ave, Wenatchee
509.888.0374; caffemela.com

Stemilt Creek Winery
110 N Wenatchee Ave., Wenatchee
509.665.3485; stemiltcreekwinery.co

Chateau Faire LePont
1 Vineyard Way, Wenatchee
509.667.9463; fairelepont.com

Your dog wants a vacation too... Bring him along!

We have 26 dog friendly hotel rooms at the Icicle Village Resort, the most in Leavenworth! And all are located on the 1st floor with easy access to our pet garden.

So yes, give your dog a vacation... Besides, we can't wait to meet him, or her!

1.800.961.0162 iciclevillage.com

Icicle Village
R E S O R T
LEAVENWORTH, WA

pet-peeps
connecting **People** with their **Pets**

Only
$99.
each

YOUR CHOICE

SEE, HEAR + TALK
to your pet from anywhere

Wireless or Wired, Pan + Tilt 360 degrees, 2 way audio, Motion detection, Records for playback, 1 yr warranty, works on any iPhone, Android, Tablet or iPad, Free tech support, Free app

Go to:
PET-PEEPS.COM

PET-PEEPS.COM
MODEL PP309BZ

pet-peeps
connecting People with their Pets

Lake Chelan

WITH 300 DAYS OF SUNSHINE LAKE CHELAN PROMISES FOUR SEASONS OF FUN WITH FIDO.

The name "Chelan" comes from the Indian word, "Salish," which means "deep water," which is appropriate considering Lake Chelan is the third deepest lake in the country, boasting 1,486 feet at its deepest point. The 50.5-mile lake is fed year round from streams that originate deep in the Cascade Mountains, and its crystal clear water makes it ideal for all sorts of activities—today, during the dog days of summer, we see people of all ages swimming, water skiing, wind surfing, sun bathing (even someone doing yoga)—Lake Chelan is a playground indeed!

There is so much to see and do here, from dining at fine restaurants to partaking in water sports, to hiking, wine tasting, and so much more. Lake Chelan is truly Washington's playground. And, what better way to enjoy a playground, than with your pooch?

STAY And, that's exactly what you should do when you arrive at **Lakeside Lodge and Suites** (your home away from home for the next two days). Lakeside Lodge (hence, its name) is literally steps away from the lake (100 yards to be exact), with a huge, grassy park at the water's edge. Dips your toes (and paws) in the cool water, then take in the breathtaking beauty of Lake Chelan before the sun sets.

Clockwise from top: Jessica and Harley cool off from the hot summer sun; enjoying a stroll along the dock at Lake Chelan; a refreshing glass of white wine at Fromaggio Bistro; John Little shares Rio Vista's Wacky White, featuring yellow Lab Rocky on the label.

Photos by Julie Clegg

GETTING HERE Follow I-90 E to WA-10/WA-970 in Kittitas County. Take exit 85 from I-90 E. Follow WA-970 to US-97 N. Follow US-97 N and US-2 E to Euclid Ave in Sunnyslope. Exit from US-2 E/US-97 N. Follow US-97 ALT N to E Johnson Avenue in Chelan.

Clockwise from top: Enjoy a glass of rosé at Hard Row to Hoe; WineGirl Wines serves up Yappy Hour every Thursday; Harley at Lakeside Lodge.

...LAY Instead of driving on your own, we recommend hiring a tour guide for the day—**Lakeside Limousine** to be exact. As your driver holds the door pile in the back with your pooch, and head to your first wine tasting excursion of the day at **Rio Vista Wines**. While you may opt to head there by limo, there is also the option of arriving by seaplane (no joke). Situated on the banks of the Columbia River, Rio Vista Wines is the only waterfront winery in the region and **Chelan Seaplanes** will whisk you there, with a 10-minute, scenic flight.

The sweeping property at Rio Vista is gorgeous—and better yet, totally dog friendly. Dogs are allowed to explore off-leash with their new pal, Rocky, the state's resident Lab and face that graces one of the winery's 11 labels, Wacky White. While the dogs venture down to the river, head to the tasting room, where you are met by winery owners John and Jan Little. The couple grows even varieties of grapes on the property, from pinot gris to gewurztraminer

(try saying that three times!) and all of them are delicious. Be sure to buy a bottle of Wacky White before embarking on your next wine tasting adventure at **Hard Row to Hoe Vineyards**.

First, a bit about the name "Hard Row to Hoe." Apparently, the monicker celebrates the entrepreneurial spirit of a man who ran a row boat taxi service on Lake Chelan in the 1930's, ferrying miners by rowboat to a brothel located at Point Lovely. It's quite a cheeky name for a seriously delicious wine, but pairs perfectly with the ambiance of the place, which embodies fun! The tasting room is a bit on the saucy side (be sure to go in for a closer look at the wall paper), with feather boas, velvet chaise lounges, and wines featuring names like "Nauti Buoy," "Double Dip" and "Seduction Red." If it's hot (no pun intended), grab a glass of chilled rosé and head outside to hang with your pooch on the lovely patio.

After Hard Row to Hoe, it's off to the **WineGirl Wines**, located back in Manson! Every Thursday during the summer, Wine Girl Wines hosts a dog-friendly Yappy Hour to help raise money for the Humane Society of Wenatchee (HSW). With a $5 donation to HSW, you get 10% off your wine by the glass plus the enjoyment of having your pooch with you. There is even a fenced area adjacent to the tasting room, where your four-legged friend can play off-leash, while you and your two-

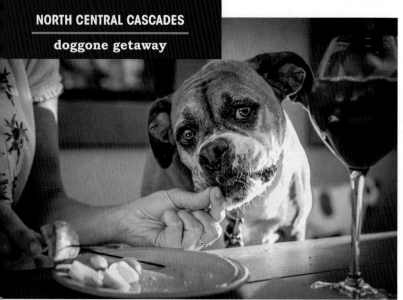

Photos by Julie Clegg

Above: Harley enjoys a nibble at Fromaggio Bistro. Left: Pick up a blueberry or apricot pie, enjoy a delicious brunch on the dog-friendly patio, or pick your own blueberries at Blueberry Hills Farms, a must-do on your visit to Lake Chelan.

Alas, if you are visiting in the summer, cool off back at the lodge by the outdoor swimming pool, before venturing out for dinner. We recommend one of the colorful picnic tables in the outside seating are at **Fromaggio Bistro**. After a long day of wine tasting, your pooch is sure to be tuckered, so after a few attempts at begging, Fido can rest their head on the cool brick patio, while you go all out with the menu. Start with the antipasto plate, with artichokes, olives, peppers, pickled asparagus and green beans, fresh caper berries, cheese and Italian meats, accompanied with a house white wine, served over ice with a slice of lime. As the name of the restaurant implies ("fromaggio" means "cheese" in Italian), there is an entire section of the menu dedicated to cheese: Cheese Fondue, Fromaggio Mac-n-Cheese, and 3-Cheese Ravioli, to name a few. While we love cheese, the Beef Medallions in a Port Mushroom Sauce are way too good to pass up!

The next morning, before heading back to Seattle, a must-do is breakfast at **Blueberry Hills Farms**. Getting there is tricky, so set your GPS before you go. As you pull into the gravel parking lot, don't be surprised by how many people are already here, with a line out the door. However, it moves quickly and before you know it, you and your pooch are comfortably seated on the outdoor patio overlooking the farm's "u-pick" blueberry fields. And, no matter the wait, with items like Kari's Blintz (one large sweet crepe

legged friends enjoy a tasting flight that includes two of the winery's whites and two of their reds—all four of them amazing, I might add.

Following wine tasting, it's a good time to take a break for lunch, and enjoy delicious sandwiches from **Village Market & Deli** in Manson. More than a market and a deli, there is also a bar, where you can taste beer from Lake Chelan Brewery, located right next door and owned by the same family.

After lunch, set out on your own to do some exploring—there is no shortage of things to do year-round in Chelan. Cooler fall temperatures make for more enjoyable hiking and the **Reach 1 Trail** offers you and Fido a 3-mile-plus round-trip walk that overlooks the Chelan Dam, Lake Chelan and the Chelan River. The trail takes you from the Riverwalk Loop Trail in downtown Chelan to Reach 1 of the Chelan River—the uppermost section of the river that joins the Columbia River at Chelan Falls. Another trail favorite among locals is Chelan Butte. There is an old road crossing the face of the Butte that is perfect for running or hiking with your hound and offers some fantastic views of the the lake.

Photo by Julie Clegg

ed with a blend of ricotta and cream cheeses, topped with your ɔice of warm pie filling: blueberry, peach, or both, and a dollop of ɪipped cream), it's worth it. After breakfast, if you feel so inclined, ɪb a bucket from the counter outside, and pick blueberries in the ɪarby field to take home with you—blueberries are $2 a pound ɪen you "u-pick."

Whether it's during the dog days of summer, or when it's a winter ɔnderland, there is no shortage of things to see and do, from water ɔrts to wine tasting, swimming to skiing, Lake Chelan offers year-ɪnd fun for you and Fido. 🐾

ɔRE INFORMATION

** keside Lodge and Suites**
l2 W Woodin Avenue, Chelan
Ɉ.682.4396; lakesidelodgeandsuites.com

ɪenities include king or double queen suites,
ɪh lake views, heated indoor pool, kitchens and
ɪnplimentary breakfast.

ɪrley and her mom relax on the dock at Lake Chelan.

Rio Vista Wines
24415 Highway #97, Chelan
509.682.9713; riovistawines.com

Hard Row to Hoe Vineyards
300 Ivan Morse Road, Manson
509.687.3000; hardrow.com

WineGirl Wines
222 E Wapato Way, Manson
509.293.9679; winegirlwines.com

Village Market & Deli
50 Wapato Way, Manson
509.687.4444

Fromaggio Bistro & Wine Bar
14 E Wapato Way, Manson
509.888.6452; fromaggiomanson.com

Blueberry Hills Farms
1315 Washington Street, Manson
509.687.2379; wildaboutberries.com

Winthrop

WINTHROP, LOCATED IN THE
METHOW VALLEY IS A MECCA
FOR OUTDOOR ENTHUSIASTS.

It's a scenic drive along Highway
20, winding through the majestic
peaks of the north Cascade
Mountains to the historic town of
Winthrop, located in the heart of
the Methow Valley.

With over 1,000 square miles of
mountain peaks, valleys, glaciers,
and wilderness, the Methow Valley
is a Mecca for outdoor enthusiasts
and dog lovers alike.

With year-round activities, the
valley draws visitors looking for
adventure from river rafting, hiking,
rock climbing and mountain biking
in the summer, to cross country
skiing and snow-shoeing in the
winter. And, no matter the time
of year, dogs are of course always
welcome in Winthrop.

Settled in the late 1800s,
Winthrop keeps its frontier past
alive with its Old West theme,
with wooden boardwalks, old
time storefronts and small town
charm, all of which is back-dropped
by mountain peaks, expansive
farmland, horse ranches, rolling
hills and a river running through it.

STAY Make your destination
in Winthrop the family-owned
Spring Creek Ranch, located at
the confluence of the Methow and
Chewuch Rivers. The ranch was
homesteaded in the late 1800s and

**Clockwise from top: Scout and Ayla
explore the grounds at Spring Creek
Ranch; Scout and Ayla; Scout relaxes
at Spring Creek Cabin; Ziggy and the
gang follow the path along Spring
Creek to the Methow River. Previous
page: Scout enjoys a scoop at Sheri's.**

GETTING HERE Take I-5 North to Arlington. Follow Hwy 530 to Hwy 20. Take Hwy 20
ast to Winthrop. Note: Hwy 20 is closed in winter, but alternate routes are available.

Photos by Julie Clegg

Clockwise from top: Spring Creek Cabin; it's comfy and cozy in the cabin's loft area; a couple of happy pups at Old Schoolhouse Brewery.

sits on 60 acres of open meadow with riverfront and trail access. There's an expansive field separating the main house from Spring Creek Cabin, where dogs can run free. Explore the trail to Spring Creek, where salmon spawn. A little further down the trail is the lovely Methow River, complete with a sitting area and hammock situated along the river's edge.

Spring Creek Cabin is roomy, with a fully stocked kitchen, bathroom, living area, gas fireplace, TV and DVD player plus a bedroom downstairs and another bedroom in the loft area. It's super cozy with a big front porch and Adirondack chairs to relax and take in the scenery. Do not be surprised if a deer or two stroll by, munching their way through the grassy meadow.

PLAY As your next order of business, be sure to swing by the **Winthrop Visitor Center**, located at the four-way intersection as you enter town, to pick up maps and information about the area. A great resource is **Methow Trails**, whose goal

is to "establish the finest and mos interesting year-round trail recreation area in the United States." W are pleasantly surprised to discov dogs are welcome on 40km of the trails, all National Forest trails and designated Wilderness Areas in the Methow Valley, adding up to miles and miles of trails for dogged exploration. If you visit the North Cascades National Park, the Methow Trails website (*methowtrails.org*) is a wealth of information including a page ded cated to dog friendly ski trails.

Of the countless trails, we recommend **Falls Creek**, where a beautiful waterfall awaits. It's a 15-minute drive from Winthrop t get there, with a short, ¼ mile hik to a beautiful waterfall — there is also a campground nearby. For more extended hikes, locals recommend **Big Valley**, located right off of Highway 20. It feature a flat, wooded trail along the rive allowing for lots of opportunities to enjoy a swim. The **Community Trail** from the nearby town of Mazama offers a pleasant hike or bike ride. Be sure to stop at the **Mazama Country Store** for yummy baked goods. The store has a dog run in the gorgeous outdoor seating area. For the mor ambitious, **Goat Peak Lookout** at 7,000 feet elevation is a great 2.5 mile hike to an old fire lookout. All of these trails can be found on the MVSTA map, so don't forget to grab one at the visitor's center before heading out with your four-legged hiking partner.

Following your visit to Falls Creek, head to **Sheri's Sweet Shoppe** for a treat. As you walk though the doors, you may spot

**Top: Scout at Spring Creek Ranch.
Above and left: Sheri's Sweet Shoppe.**

SIT If by now you are starving, head back into town to the **Old Schoolhouse Brewery** for a burger and a beer. There is a huge, riverside deck area and if you are lucky enough to grab a table near the outside perimeter, your dogs can be with you as long as they stay on the outside of the railing. Perusing the menu, the "No Cheese Left Behind Nachos" might sound tempting, but you can't go wrong with Casey's Classic Burger topped with grilled onions and mushrooms, Swiss cheese, and a special Casey's Beer Sauce, or the Wrangler Burger with apple-smoked bacon, grilled onions, cheddar cheese, and BBQ sauce. Delicious.

More dining options include **Arrowleaf Bistro** and **East 20 Pizza**. Arrowleaf Bistro, named for the native wildflower that grows in the region, blends regional favorites and locally produced products with the tenets of classic bistro cooking including organic, pasture-raised beef and chicken sourced from local ranches. For pizza lovers, East 20 Pizza is almost worth the entire four-hour drive to Winthrop for a little slice of heaven.

After a peaceful night's sleep back at the cabin, it's up and at 'em for another full day of exploring. The Methow Valley offers so many things to see, do, eat and drink that we recommend at least four days to squeeze

op owner Tate Johnston stirring a copper pot full of caramel for a tray of ranny Smith apples sitting nearby. After you've taken in the sights and nells, head to the expansive deck, with tables and a fresh water station for e dogs, a pee wee golf course, and best of all, an ice cream stand. More eats include Milk Bones dipped in doggy-safe white chocolate for the ooches and a plethora of sweets for the peeps.

Next, meander over to a nearby park situated at the edge of the Methow iver to cool off and watch as paddle boarders and rafters float by. The park is cated next to The Barn, a community center for meetings, dances and events.

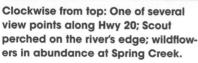

Photos by Julie Clegg

Clockwise from top: One of several view points along Hwy 20; Scout perched on the river's edge; wildflowers in abundance at Spring Creek.

it all in. Start the day at **Rocking Horse Bakery**, where they offer freshly baked handcrafted goodies, including artisan breads and bagels, decadent pastries, mouthwatering scones and muffins, and specialty cakes, pies and cookies. Gourmet soups, sandwiches, salads and pizza are made from scratch daily and feature many local ingredients. Be sure to try their 100% organic, fair trade coffee and espresso roasted locally in Winthrop by **Backcountry Coffee Roasters**.

Be sure to check out the **Schafer Historical Museum** for a glimpse into the region's past. This popular Old West museum features a collection of pioneer nostalgia and historic buildings including "The Castle," built in 1897 by Winthrop founder Guy Waring as a log home for he and his wife.

PLAY If visiting Winthrop during the summer, **Pearrygin Lake State Park** is a popular destination for cooling off, whether its swimming, jet skiing,

kayaking, canoeing or fishing for rainbow trout. The park features boat launch, dock, parking for RV as well as tent sites, and a roped-swimming area.

July to October is also prime mountain biking season in the Methow Valley, with a range of options for experts, beginners and everyone in between. Locals recommend **Sun Mountain** for beginners and experts alike, **Buck Mountain** for a bit more technical ride, and for riders looking for a challenge, **Angels Staircase** climb to 8,200 feet for an all-day pedal over mountain passes.

If you enjoy wine, **Lost River Winery**, a boutique family-owned winery, located at 26 Hwy 10 near Winthrop, produces wines like Cedarosa, Community Red, Nebbiolo, Pinot Gris and Massif that have received notable award The winery's tasting room is open on Thursday through Monday, year round from 11 a.m. to 5 p.m. and well-socialized dogs are welcome. There is also a dog hitch and water bowls outside.

If you are visiting the Valley over a weekend, be sure to hit the Saturday Farmers Market in Twisp and the Sunday Farmers Market in Winthrop. The **Twisp Farmers Market** is considered one of the best in the state, offering everything from veggies and greens in the spring to pumpkins and potatoes in the fall—all for the past 30-plus years. Items have to be handmade and sold by the person who makes them, locally-grown and sold by the person who grows them, or items with added value such as jam made from fruit

...om left: **Winthrop harkens back to the Old West; stopping to enjoy the majestic waterfall at Fall Creek Trail.**

...urchased by another grower. ...he market also features live ...usic and kids' activities such as ...e famous zucchini races.

Also during summer months, ...e Methow Valley is home to ...number of festivals including ...e Winthrop Wine Festival, ...ethow Arts Festival, Winthrop ...hythm & Blues Festival and ...e North Cascades Oldtime ...iddlers Contest.

Although there is an ...ncredible amount to see and do ...uring the dog days of summer, ...e must not forget winter in ...Vinthrop. The Methow Valley ...s a maze of backcountry ...rails for Nordic skiing and ...nowshoeing. In fact, strap on ...our skis or snowshoes, grab ...he dog and head out right from ...pring Creek Cabin to find ...roomed trails literally at your ...ront door. Methow Trails also ...ecommends these dog friendly

jaunts: **Lunachick Trail**, a 1.6 kilometer trail accessed at the Edelweiss camping area parking lot (multi-use for walking, snowshoeing and skiing and no trail pass is needed), **Big Valley Trail**, with four and eight kilometer loops (multi-use and no trail pass is needed), and the **Rendezvous System** with 46.9 kilometers of trails (ski only, a trail pass is needed, and access the dog trail from Cub Creek).

No matter the time of year, Winthrop and the Methow Valley will have your adventure hound howling with glee! Take your time and stop at one or all of the scenic viewpoints along the way. The scenery is just about the best of any highway anywhere.

During the winter months (usually November to April), Hwy 20 is closed, so take I-5 North to Hwy 2/Stevens Pass through Leavenworth or I-90 East/Snoqualmie Pass to Blewett Pass. Call 800.695.ROAD or visitwsdot.wa.gov/traffic/passes for current conditions. 🐾

MORE INFORMATION

Spring Creek Ranch
7 Johnson Lane
Winthrop, Wash.
509.996.2495
springcreekwinthrop.com

Winthrop Visitor Center
At the corner of Hwy 20 and Riverside Ave.
888.463.8469; winthropwashington.com

Methow Valley Sport Trails Association
509.996.3287; mvsta.com

Mazama

A MUTT-FRIENDLY GATEWAY TO THE NORTH CASCADES AND THE GREAT OUTDOORS.

Follow highway 20 east through Washington state's North Cascades mountain range, and you'll descend a scenic and winding road that courses through the Methow Valley, with its breathtaking natural beauty, unlike any place you've ever seen. Statuesque pine trees follow the route made by the mighty Methow River, and the 200 kilometer long trail system awaits your summer time biking, horseback riding, hiking, rock-climbing and fishing adventures. Make sure to pack your gear and everything you'll need for your pup, as this place is dog friendly — *really* dog friendly.

STAY Decline through the rocky, jutted mountains and you'll settle into the lush valley where you'll find yourself in a little town called Mazama. Blink and you'll miss it. So try not to blink or you'll drive past the majestic timber-framed lodge known as Freestone Inn. The main building at Freestone houses luxury suites, and there are 15 rustic, yet stylish cabins scattered throughout the lodge's pine tree lined roads. Leash up Fido and meander along one of the trails to the main lodge where you and your pup can enjoy award winning food al fresco style. Dogs are welcome at the lodge's Sandy Butte Bistro & Bar's spacious outdoor patio with its magnificent and sweeping view of the mountains. Don't forget a towel for your pup, who will most definitely want to take a dip in the one-acre lake just steps away from restaurant. "Dogs love to swim in our lake," says Jojo Howard of Freestone Inn, "that, and chase the squirrels!"

Research the area before you take the drive over to the Methow Valley, where there are a number of dog-friendly hotels and cabins available for rent. Freestone Inn is a favorite due to how they welcome pups as a part of the family, with fresh water bowls and special order pup meals available, the staff warmly encourages guests and their dogs to join in exploring the grounds, trails, and many of the lodge's amenities together. Wherever you decide to rest your head at night, make sure to get a good night's sleep because big morning adventure awaits you in this jewel of a small mountain town.

**Previous page: Hanging at on the porch at the Freestone Inn.
Above: Play time at the lake on the Freestone Inn property.**

LAY Wake rested, leash up your pooch and head out on a hike on one of the many dog-friendly routes in the Methow Trails. Made up of connected landscapes, the trails run the gamut from flat, leisurely strolls to multi-day hike-in and hike-out options and everything in-between. Many routes are wheel-chair accessible, and often times you'll pass mountain bike riders, horseback riders, and birders trying to get a glimpse of the hundred of species of birds who frequent the area.

Make sure to bring water and eats for both you and your dog, and if you forgot them, never fear just swing in to the dog-friendly Mazama Store, where you can get 'a little bit of everything good.'

If you'd rather take your pup for a river rafting ride, you can do that too, there are a number of rafting companies in the area. Just make sure the river is calm and you and your dog wear floatation devices. If fishing is your thing, know the rules of the river, cast away and soon you and your pup will be dining on some of the best catch in the Pacific Northwest. Whatever your outdoor pleasure, the Methow Valley has it in spades, including photography. You certainly don't want to miss all of the fun selfie moments with you and your fuzzy best friend.

SIT When you get hungry and need a little break, drive east toward the cowboy-themed town of Winthrop. A relatively new restaurant addition to the area, the Methow Valley Ciderhouse is waiting to serve you and your pup. The Methow Valley Ciderhouse has room for 50 people on their dog-friendly deck and will add seating for another 100 this summer, as well as an outdoor dance floor, a bocce ball court and other outdoor games. "We cater to families and offer local artisan sausages, a kid friendly menu, with vegan and gluten free options," says Lynne Wasson, owner of the Methow Valley Ciderhouse. "We have seven ciders on tap, plus five beers and offer wine, and free dog training advice since I am one of two resident dog trainers in the Methow Valley."

If you feel like heading a little further on Highway 20 you can drive the 20 minutes to Twisp, where you can visit the dog-friendly TwispWorks campus and experience a lovely incubation of local artisans, craftspeople and producers creating Methow made goods.

When you are out in nature, taking in all of its glory like the kind the Methow Valley area offers, it doesn't really matter what the day holds in store for you. All that really counts is that you have your fuzzy best friend by your side. So go out and explore the beauty of the area, and when you have had your fill and need a cool dip, spread a blanket out on a shady spot along the river bank, and make time for you and your pup to enjoy a refreshing dip in the crisp, clear Methow River. Your dog will love it! 🐾

MORE INFORMATION

Freestone Inn
31 Early Winters Drive, Mazama.
509.996.3906; freestoneinn.com

The Mazama Store
50 Lost River Road, Mazama
509.996.2855; themazamastore.com

Methow Valley Ciderhouse
28 State Hwy 20, Winthrop
methowvalleyciderhouse.com

TwispWorks
502 South Glover Street, Twisp
509.997.3300; twispworks.org

Photo by Teri Pieper

Washington Wine Country

The Columbia, Yakima and Walla Walla Valleys offer world class wines and dog-friendly wineries...perfect for oenohiles and dog lovers alike.

hoto by Julie Austin

ANY PET PHOTOGRAPHY

I capture you & your pet's wonderful, wild, crazy, playful, unconditional love.

Come play at the beach!
Mini Sessions in
Seabrook , Washington!
June 9th & 10th
See website for details.

Voted Evening Magazine's
"The Best of Western Washington"

Best Pet Photography
6 Years in a row, 2012 - 2017!

www.jaustinphotography.com | 425.802.3944

NITRO K-9 LLC

EUROPEAN DOG TRAINING WITH

AN EASTERN TWIST

Private Behavior Modification Since 1994

- Specializing In Aggression and Anxiety
- Obedience On and Off Leash
- Discounts for Police and Military
- Protection Dogs | Service Dogs

OBEDIENCE, PROTECTION AND SERVICE DOGS

www.nitrocanine.com | (206) 412-9979

Photos by Julie Clegg

ONE OF THE MOST GLORIOUS THINGS ABOUT WASHINGTON IS THE ABUNDANCE OF FIRST-CLASS WINERIES. TRAVERSING THE STATE WITH YOUR DOG FOR A LITTLE WINE TASTING IS A PERFECT WAY TO SPEND THE DAY, A WEEKEND, OR EVEN AN EXTENDED VACATION.

According to the Washington State Wine Commission, Washington wines are a $4.8 billion dollar industry, and Washington state is the second largest premium wine producer in the United States. Every year sixty thousand glorious acres of fertile Washington land, lovingly tended by passionate grape growers, result in 14.8 million cases of wine.

Of the 900 plus wineries in Washington state, 25 percent are located in the Tri-Cities, Walla Walla Valley, and Yakima Valley area. This region, commonly referred to as Washington Wine Country, has the ideal climate, soil, and elevation for wine grape growing and was the first American Vitaculture Area in the state of Washington.

With over 240 wineries in the region, you are sure to enjoy your visit to Washington Wine Country. You'll come for the wine, and stay for the beauty. Blessed each year with nearly 300 days of sunshine, this area attracts many top-notch chefs, vibrant merchants, and service-oriented hoteliers. Wherever you go in Washington Wine Country you are sure to be catered to and made to feel like an honored guest.

Be sure to bring Fido too, as Washington Wine Country is known for being dog-friendly. Many of the area's tasting rooms have their own 'winery dog' to greet you and four-legged visitors too. Well-mannered dogs of all sizes are welcomed at numerous wineries, outdoor restaurants, coffee shops, retail establishments, resorts, and nightly rentals.

Pepper Fewel, owner of Cherry Wood Bed, Breakfast and Barn, and her three rescues Jessie (left), Peewee (center) and Stuka (right); Cooper at the head of the Cowiche Canyon Trail near Yakima.

Walla Walla

WALLA WALLA WILL LEAVE YOU AND YOUR PUP 'WANNA-WANNA-ING' FOR MORE.

With rolling hills welcoming you to Walla Walla, you'll be excited to see all that the region has to offer a first-time visitor, as well as the experienced returning guest. If you are a novice to the area, you will be amazed at how dog-friendly Walla Walla is, so make sure to bring along your dog's favorite toys, a chew stick, and water bowl with you as you embark on your food, wine and tourist adventure!

STAY Your first order of business is to find a place to stay. While there are numerous dog-friendly chain and local hotels, the **Marcus Whitman Hotel** is a welcoming place to lay your head and your pup's dog bed which is provided by the hotel if needed.

Built as a labor of love by the community in 1928, the 133-room Marcus Whitman, named in honor of an early missionary who helped establish the region, was and still is one of Walla Walla's most popular gathering places, with a fine dining restaurant, four tasting rooms, an art gallery, conference center and even an outdoor, grassy play area for your pooch, complete with potty station. The rooms are elegant yet accessible, clearly nothing to sniff at, with beautifully crafted furnishings, plush beds, comfy down pillows, premium linens, large flat screen televisions, free WiFi, and numerous amenities.

Photos by Julie Austin

Clockwise from top: Winery dog Lucy greets visitors to Va Piano Vineyards; hors d'oeuvres at Brasserie Four; enjoy a picnic lunch from Olive Marketplace; bottles at Dunham Cellars; the chefs at Brasserie Four prepare delicious French cuisine.

GETTING HERE Follow I-90 E to WA-26 E in Grant County. Take exit 137 from I-90 E. Follow WA-243 S and WA-240 E to I-182 E in Richland. Merge onto I-182 E Follow US-12 E to N 5th Ave to downtwon Walla Walla.

Photos by Julie Austin

LAY Nestled in the heart of the historic area of downtown Walla Walla, e Marcus Whitman is within walking distance to numerous wine tasting oms, and surrounded by hundreds of wineries within a very short drive. e Walla Walla Valley is divided into six regions, each one home to ozens of wineries. One area to explore is the Airport Region, named for location near the airport, with the first stop starting at **Dunham Cellars,** hich makes its home in some of the hangars in the area.

In just over a matter of decades, the Walla Walla Valley has emerged as e of the the premier wine destinations of the world, and one of the first the scene was Dunham. When Dunham's first vintage was released, 1995 Cabernet Sauvignon, it was deemed one of the finest wines ade in Washington by Wine Enthusiast Magazine. Of course, CityDog agazine's favorite Dunham Cellars wines have dogs on the labels and clude their delicious **Three Legged Red**, which features former winery og and 'tri-pawed' Port on the label, and **Four Legged White**, which atures winery dog Maysy (pictured above with fellow winery dog die). As you can tell Dunham Cellars loves dogs, and be ready to be eeted by their winery dogs upon arrival. Take your time and explore e wines served in flights or in singular tastes, and bring a few Walla alla inspired treats to taste while you enjoy your stay and learn about unham's wines and their dogs.

Another tasty stop in the Airport Region is **Adamant Cellars**. Established 2006, Adamant's winemaker and owners, Devin and Debra Stinger, are ssionate about making incredibly crafted, outstanding wines. This dedica-n shows in the Adamant Cellars merlot, syrah, and cabernet sauvignon.

bove from left: Winery dogs Maysy (left) and Sadie (right) at unham Cellars; hanging out at the Marcus Whitman Hotel.

SIT One of the most convenient things about Walla Walla wine tasting is the layout of the regions and how easy it is to return to the downtown area for a quick snack or to gather food for a picnic basket while you make your way to the next winery. Be sure to stop at **Olive Marketplace & Cafe** on East Main Street in downtown Walla Walla.

With its outdoor patio seating, Olive is a perfect place for you and your pup to sit, sip, and nosh, and if you're in a hurry you can always just grab a delicious turkey club, with smoked bacon, fontina, tomato, greens, avocado and basil aioli on seeded wheat bread, to go. If vegetarian is more your style, try the veggie sandwich packed with creamy hummus and avocado, delicately roasted vegetables, on sweet smelling wheat bread.

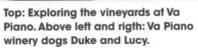
Top: Exploring the vineyards at Va Piano. Above left and rigth: Va Piano winery dogs Duke and Lucy.

PLAY After noshing, head down to **Va Piano Vineyards,** "go slow" in Italian, in the Southside Region, where the bulk of the vineyards are located. Open seven days a week, Va Piano has been home to five generations of a wine making family called the Wylies.

The Va Piano estate is gorgeous, with a Tuscan-styled tasting room, surrounded by lush vineyards. Your stop would not be complete without chatting with Justine Wylie, Va Piano's winemaker and Chief Relaxation Officer, to learn about the ecological features of the area and how they affect the wines. Va Piano's wines are reflective of bold elegance of the Walla Walla area, creating quality products from accessible everyday drinking wine to small-lot, estate-style wines. On a hot summer day, you'll welcome a taste of Va Piano's French Creek Vineyard Chardonnay with its subtly endearing pear, melon, and tropical fruity flavors. The well cared for tasting room

grounds of Va Piano invite you to sit and stay a while, so bring a blanket for you to sit on and a ball for your dog to chase with the playful and friendly winery dogs Duke and Lucy.

A half-mile down the road from Va Piano, be sure to stop by **Saviah Cellars,** where winemaker and owner Richard Funk will give you a tour and provide you with some tastes of their award winning wines. Starting out small in 2000, producing 300 cases of wine Saviah Cellars has grown to 25,00 cases annually.

Saviah welcomes dogs and even has treats for them upon arriving at the tasting room. Like many Washington wines, Saviah flavors are richly terroir driven, where a a mix of soil, earth, clima and weather combine to provide a deep, layered taste. A definite must-taste is the Tempranillo. Deep ruby in color, it bursts with juicy, spicy essence with a hint of pepper and tobacco, and offers a smoothness that balances it all ou

Next, head north back toward town, and stop at **Bergevin Lane Winery** to meet founding partner Annette Bergevin, tastin room manager Julie Myrick, and winery dogs Paco, Fergie and Cody. Paco, a Chihuahua-rat terrier mix, is clearly the boss of the bunch, so make sure to say hello and allow your dog to politely check-in with the pack. The brick building feels nice and cool on a hot summer day, and with all of the pups making nice you can take your time to chat with Julie about the wonderful wines that Bergevin has to offer.

Photos by Julie Austin

Photos by Julie Austin

The 90 point She-Devil Syrah is a favorite with its silky dark fruit, and t the right hint of smoke and earth make this a must taste wine. Another : to miss sip, the Moonspell Cabernet Sauvignon is another 90 point ne that Bergevin Lane Winery has crafted to just the right blend of ckberries and cherries, spices, and cassis.

Next, stop at **Saffron Mediterranean Kitchen** on West Main in ılla Walla's downtown district, and within walking distance from the ırcus Whitman Hotel. Owned by Chris and Island Ainsworth and their odesian ridgeback Elvis, Saffron offers first-come, first-serve outdoor ting for you and your dog. The Mediterranean-inspired dishes like opus, paella negra, linguini, razor clam flatbread, falafel, and bastilla, ng with craft cocktails, and an expansive beer and wine list are azing. After dinner you may want—or perhaps need—to go for a walk he downtown core, where window shopping is plentiful, and you can oy the beautiful music seeping outdoors from the nightspots that you lk by on your way back to the hotel.

AY Fresh from a good night's sleep in your plush bed with down lows and luxurious linens, and maybe after a quick work out in the ıess center, leash up your dog and drive to nearby **Bennington Lake** for ttle exploration. Bennington Lake is the perfect place for Walla Walla als and their pooches to enjoy the great outdoors without having to out of town. The area includes more than 20 miles of trails through ın grasslands and wooded areas set against the backdrop of the Blue untains. It also includes Rooks Park, an 18-acre park with picnic tables, yground, volleyball court, horseshoe pit, barbeque grills and more.

ove from left: Chris and Island Ainsworth's former Rhodesian gebacks, painted by Leiv Fanereng; their current pup, Elvis.

Best of all, dogs are welcome at the Bennington Lake area, as well as in the park and on the trails. Be sure to pick up a map at the US Army Corps of Engineers Mill Creek Office (3211 Reservoir Road, Walla Walla) in order to locate the designated on-leash and off-leash areas as you explore the area.

As you head back to downtown, for your last day of wine tasting, noshing, and having fun with Fido, make sure to swing by **Wags to Whiskers**. This Walla Walla premier pet store carries a variety of dog food, including refrigerated and frozen raw, has a natural bulk bar with nearly 30 different types of dog treats, and even offers a do-it-yourself dog wash to get your pup all spiffed up from their Bennington Lake excursion.

With your pup all clean, treated, and exercised it's time to try a few

Photos by Julie Austin

Clockwise from top: Enjoying a run at Bennington Lake; Annette Bergevin and Fergie; a delicious starter at Saffron Mediterranean Kitchen.

escargots in garlic and parsley butter, Assiette de Fromage selection of imported cheeses, and Caesar salad, followed by steak frites of hanger steak with fries and cognac black pepper cream sauce, and end the meal with chocolate mousse and a dollop of creme fraiche. Délicieux! 🐾

MORE INFORMATION

Marcus Whitman Hotel
6 West Rose Street
Reservations: 866.826.9422
marcuswhitmanhotel.com

Rates start at $140; $35 per pet fee

Saffron Mediterranean Kitchen
125 West Alder Street
saffronmediterraneankitchen.com

Dunham Cellars
150 East Boeing Avenue
dunhamcellars.com

Adamant Cellars
525 East Cessna Avenue
adamantcellars.com

Olive Marketplace & Cafe
21 East Main Street
olivemarketplaceandcafe.com

Va Piano Vineyards
1793 JB George Road
vapianovineyards.com

Saviah Cellars
1979 JB George Road
saviahcellars.com

Bergevin Lane Vineyards
1215 West Poplar Street
bergevinlane.com

Brasserie Four
4 East Main Street

Wags to Whiskers
301 East Main Street

Bennington Lake
3211 Reservoir Road

of the tasting rooms in downtown Walla Walla. You don't have to go far for your afternoon sips—literally, just steps outside the door of the Marcus Whitman are some of the best wineries in the country, maybe even the world.

Pick up a downtown Walla Walla tourist map from the hotel and on it you'll find walking directions to **Lagana Cellars**, **Cuneo Cellars**, **Henry Earl Estate Wines**, **Kontos Cellars**, and **Spring Valley Vineyard** just to name a few. Let your curiosity, and your nose be your guide, and enjoy what the numerous large and small tasting rooms have to offer.

SIT For your last dinner in Walla Walla, try something truly divine—namely, **Brasserie Four**. While the restaurant's interior is not dog friendly, the lovely outside patio is and well behaved dogs are definitely welcome.

As soon as you walk through the door of this fine French restaurant, you know you are in for a special treat. Start off with a few of their specialities like

Yakima Valley

JUST A THREE-HOUR DRIVE EAST FROM SEATTLE SITS THE GLORIOUS YAKIMA VALLEY.

On your way into Yakima, heading west to east, make a must-stop-and-see at the Yakima Greenway, fondly known as 'The Jewel of Yakima.' The Yakima Greenway features ten miles of paved pathway, three parks, two fishing lakes, four river access landings with protected and natural areas, and a fully-fenced, off-leash area for your furry friend. It's the perfect place to spend a good part of your day with your dog, whether you enjoy walking, bird watching, fishing, running, biking, skating, picnicking or simple solitude. The Greenway serves as a great stop to stretch your legs and exercise your pooch before heading into Yakima Valley wine country.

STAY The Yakima Valley is the perfect hub for horse and hound lovers alike. If you also love wine, then you have found nirvana. Nirvana is a strong word, but here at CityDog Magazine we love dogs, horses, and wine and when we have all three… Nirvana! At **Cherry Wood Bed Breakfast and Barn**, near Zillah off of Interstate 82, located in the heart of the Yakima Valley's wine country, you will have all three, as well as luxury teepees. Have we blown your mind yet?

Clockwise from top: Cooper checks out the teepee at Cherry Wood Bed, Breakfast & Barn; one of Cherry Wood's rescue horses; enjoy a stroll along 10 miles of paved pathway through the Greenway; wine at Wilridge; a vintage gas station in Zillah.

ETTING HERE Follow I-90 E and I-82 E/US-97 S to Yakima. Take exit 31A-31B from I-82 'US-97 S. Continue onto N 1st St to downtown Yakima.

Photos by Julie Clegg

Left: Wine tasting at Naches Heights Vineyard. Above: Even Cooper can't resist the gelato at Russillo's Pizza and Gelato, located on the board-walk at the historic Track 29.

chicken, tomatoes, egg, bleu cheese and bacon, or a delicious seared sesame seed encrusted ahi tuna salad with wasabi cucumber dressing, or try one of their juicy hamburgers or tasty veggie burgers served with french fries. Second Street Grill has so many options that finding just one thing to try will be a challenge, but never fear they offer doggy bags for leftovers.

PLAY With full bellies you are fueled for a good work out, so opt for a hike with your dog at the **Cowiche Creek Conservancy**. Located six miles northwest of downtown Yakima, Cowiche Creek Conservancy boasts 5,000 acres, winding between the towering cliffs of the Cowiche Canyon. The former railroad line that once serviced the area now provides close to 30 miles of unpaved trails, framed with basalt and andesite rock as it meanders through sage and grasslands, and a variety of meadows while making nine crossings of the Cowiche Creek, home to salmon, beavers, crayfish, heron, and other wildlife drawn to this special climate. From where the Conservancy sits at its high point located atop Cowiche Knoll you can take a break to enjoy the 360 degree view of the Valley and the surrounding hilltops. While you could easily spend a full day exploring the Conservancy, remember there's wine to taste at the many dog-friendly wineries.

Just a 20 minute drive west will have you enjoying the views on highway 12 along your drive to **Wilridge Vineyard**. Among the vineyard's 85 acres, is a 1900s era farm house which houses the winery's entire

Cherry Wood's claim to fame is luxury, and with their dog-friendly teepees and there's no 'ruffing' it here. Each 22 foot teepee is outfitted in classic Western fare, with a queen-size, cushy bed, piled high with Pendleton wool blankets, fluffy comforters, and down pillows. Each teepee area has its own barbeque grill, compact refrigerator, bathroom area, and open-air shower. Don't let the luxury fool you, Cherry Wood is also a working farm, home to numerous horses, of which many are rescues. Owners Pepper and Terry Fewel, along with their rescue dogs, own Cherry Wood, and run it with love and passion for the land, animals, and people. Their main enterprise is farming, with acres of apple and cherry orchards surrounding the property, but, not to worry they won't put you to work. You and your pooch can go to Cherry Wood with the only goal of being to be totally pampered.

SIT Before you get too cozy at the bed and breakfast, grab some lunch at **Second Street Grill** located in downtown Yakima in a brick and timber building with a large outdoor seating area that welcomes well behaved dogs. With a big day planned that includes hiking, horseback riding, wine tasting, and walking, settle for something healthy and filling from the Second Street menu. Indulge in a BLT or avocado sandwich, or a cobb salad piled high with

eup. The tasting room
o serves as a cooperative
Washington wineries,
th dozens of other labels
taste. Also, Wilridge was
e first certified organic
d biodynamic vineyard.
odynamic farming is
generative, holistic,
ological, and ethical,
d is said to produce
ique fruits that produce
ceptional wine. Speaking
start your tasting with a
lridge pinot grigio, with
crisp and clean, tropical
rus flavor it's just the
ght beginning to pique
ur palate. Next, try the
anache rosé, followed by
medium-bodied nebbiolo.
ve some sips as your next
neyard stop is less than

Cooper enjoys the teepee's queen-size bed piled high with Pendleton blankets.

half mile south on Ehler Road. Arriving at
ches Heights Vineyards you'll see that
ey lovingly use organic and biodynamic
actices in their goal to leave the world a
tter place than it was when they got there.

The vibe at Naches Heights Vineyards
HV) is spa-like, with a tasting room
aturing an indoor/outdoor fireplace and
mfy leather sofas. Outside, the grounds
e beautiful with seating areas on the patio
xt to a waterfall, or under a pergola near
e vineyard. Wherever you sit will be a
ast for your eyes, and if you accompany
e view with a taste of NHV's gold medal
vard-winning Albarino, you will not be
ssapointed. This Spanish-style white wine
stes of peach and apricot and is perfectly
lanced on the tongue. Perhaps Two Danc-
s, a wine composed of 70 percent syrah and
percent cabernet Franc is more your style.
hichever wines you choose to taste, don't
el rushed, take your time and luxuriate in
e beautiful Naches Heights Vineyards.

SIT When you are ready to head back to town for a bite to eat,
stop in at **Russillo's Pizza and Gelato**, an authentic New York-
style pizzeria, featuring Washington wines, a full bar, classic and
gourmet pizzas, pastas, sandwiches, salads and, the highly recommended homemade gelato. Select the 'bambino-size' gelato—two
scoops of creamy goodness—then enjoy a stroll along the historic
Front Street section of downtown Yakima. This area is known for
hosting outdoor celebrations, parades, bands and festivals, so time
your visit accordingly if you want to participate in some good,
wholesome fun.

After your stroll, head back to Cherry Wood Bed Breakfast and
Barn for some rest and relaxation before dinner. Cherry Wood is
located near Zillah, a quaint town of approximately 3,100 residents
which lies just on the outskirts of the Rattlesnake Hills American
Viticultural Area. The area is simply stunning, and a leisurely
drive is a must to allow time to admire the surrounding landscape.
Approaching Cherry Wood, take note of the teepees dotting the
horizon, likely not something you see every day. Follow the signs
that point to "Teepees," your home away from home for the night.
The grounds at Cherry Wood also feature an outside seating area
and firepit, barbecue, and outdoor claw foot tubs for a soak under
the stars. Visit with the Cherry Wood horses before heading out to
dinner in nearby Sunnyside.

Photo by Julie Clegg

Photos by Julie Clegg

Left and above: Just one of many dog-friendly wineries in the Yakima Valley, Cultura, located in Zillah near Cherry Wood, is one of our favorites.

the countryside ot nearby wineries. At its core, Cherry Wood's mission is to rescue and rehabilitate abandoned and neglected horses. Once returned back to health, each horse is evaluated for inclusion in its wine tours. It's a win-win since most seem to thoroughly enjoy their semi-retirement at Cherry Wood, where they are well cared for, and receive extra attention and treats from guests. If you choose the horseback riding tour, just note that dogs need to stay behind for safety reasons. So, if you want to take Fido, the walking tour is a great way to stretch your legs and taste wine along the way. Just be sure to take plenty of water for you and your pup.

It's a short drive to **Snipes Mountain Brewery**, a family-owned restaurant and brewery with a lodge-like atmosphere — tall ceilings, rustic wood beams and a giant rock wall fireplace. Snipes has an expansive dog-friendly outdoor seating area where you can enjoy one of their many fine handcrafted, small-batch microbrews while sampling baked brie with roasted garlic, Caesar salad, pork tenderloin medallions with apple Dijon sauce, New York steak with caramelized onions, a wood fired pizzs, or gourmet burger. Wherever your stomach guides you on the menu, make sure to to save room for s'mores back at Cherry Wood — you will find all of the fixings at your teepee, along with firewood to build your campfire under the stars.

STAY It's hard to imagine that sleeping in a teepee could be so relaxing, but with the quiet of the countryside, the cool night and starry skies will have you snuggled in your cozy bed in not time. Waking refreshed and ready for more wine tasting, start the day with a delicious breakfast prepared by Cherry Wood staff, featuring Swedish pancakes with lingonberries, scrambled eggs, thick cut bacon, fresh squeezed orange juice and of course, coffee, all served on the patio overlooking the farm. Following breakfast, it's time to decide how to wine taste for the day — by car, by foot or by horse (yes, by horse). Cherry Wood offers a horseback wine tasting tour, where guests take a leisurely ride through

PLAY Cherry Wood serves as a great launching point for wine tasting. The first stop is **Cultura**, located adjacent to the farm and owned by Tad and Sarah Fewel. Cultura specializes in fine red wines, producing under 1,000 cases per year — their motto is 'quality over quantity.' Enjoy the coolness of the cement floor in their unique tasting room while you enjoy small-lot wines of bourdeaux style reds, cabernet sauvignon, merlot, zinfandel and cabernet Franc. Speaking of cab-Franc, we highly recommend their flagship wine, Kairos, a delicious blend of merlot and cabernet Franc.

From Cultura, move on to **Paradisos del Sol**, an organic, zero-pesticide, wine estate, owned by master winegrower Paul Vandenberg. The winery is family-dog-, bicycle- and horse-friendly, and you will often see all of the above on site

Photos by Julie Clegg

Above: The Yakima Valley is the perfect hub for horse and hound lovers alike. And, if you also happen to love wine, then you have found Nirvana. Right: One of the Fewel's rescue dogs, Peewee.

In Spanish, Paradisos del Sol means 'gardens of the sun,' and this little piece of paradise is perfect for wine tasting with your pooch. The tasting room is connected to the main residence and has stunning views of both Mt. Adams and Mt. Rainier, and is home to numerous friendly dogs, chickens, sheep, pigs, turkeys and other animals who help make the winery fun and interactive for both you and your pup.

On your visit, try the Seve, made from chenin blanc as well as Paradisos Red, a flavorful mix of sangiovese, malbec and cabernet sauvignon. If dessert wine is to your liking, opt for a taste of Angelica MRS, a perfectly smooth blend of semillon, riesling and a variety of muscats.

After Paradisos, head up the road to **Silverlake Winery**, where you can enjoy dramatic views from their 'viniferanda' positioned high above the vineyard to provide sweeping views of the valley below. There are also numerous shady spots for you and your pup to sit, sip, and nosh on eats. Founded in 1989, Silverlake Winery is one of the largest, locally and consumer-owned wineries in the United States, known for harvesting grapes grown in a very special location, with a protected microclimate that consistently produces ripe, balanced grapes of different varieties including cabernet sauvignon, riesling, merlot and chardonnay amongst many others. Take time to walk around the expansive vineyard, eat from the food truck typically located onsite or from the picnic snacks you brought along with you, and chat with the winemaker and wonderful people who tend to the grapevines.

For a little variety, take the seven-mile drive south and head to **Toppenish**, a community of approximately 9,000 people located entirely within the bounds of the Yakama Indian Nation. The town's pride and joy is the 75 outdoor, historical murals painted by professional artists, covering almost every available exterior wall space of the town and lends to its Old West charm. Each mural tells a story of early development of Toppenish, and its rich history and cultural diversity. Toppenish's average of 300 days of sunshine makes it a great place to visit with your pooch.

After Toppenish, head back towards Yakima and take a stop at Wapato. Once there, visit **Imperial's Garden**, a locally-owned multi-generational family farm named after the Imperial family, and a fixture in the community for the past 22 years.

Photo by Julie Clegg

Imperial's Garden does a robust business on its 1,000 acres from its first offerings of asparagus in mid-April, to its last pumpkin harvested in late October. Depending on the season, you will find snap peas, beets, onions, garlic, squash, beans, corn and Wapato sweet onions.

Alas, all good things must come to an end. Before packing up and heading out on your next adventure, say farewell to all of the new friends you made at Cherry Wood Bed, Breakfast & Barn, two- and four-legged alike! 🐾

MORE INFORMATION

Cherry Wood Bed, Breakfast & Barn
3271 Roza Drive, Zillah
509.829.3500; cherrywoodbbandb.com

Second Street Grill
28 N. 2nd Street, Yakima
509.469.1486; secondstreetgrill.com

Wilridge Vineyard
250 Ehler Road, Yakima; 509.966.0686
thetastingroomyakima.com

Naches Heights Vineyard
2410 Naches Heights Rd., Yakima
509.945.4062; nachesheights.com

Russillo's Pizza and Gelato
1 W. Yakima Ave., Suite 4, Yakima
509.453.0295; russillospizza.com

Snipes Mountain Brewery
905 Yakima Valley Hwy., Sunnyside
509.837.2739; snipesmountain.com

Imperial's Garden
4817 Lateral A Road, Wapato

Cultura Winery
3601 Highland Drive, Zillah
509.829.0204; culturawine.com

Paradisos del Sol Winery
3230 Highland Drive, Zillah
509.829.9000; paradisosdelsol.com

Toppenish Chamber of Commerce
504 South Elm, Toppenish
509.829.3262; toppenish.net

Silverlake Winery
1500 Vintage Road, Zillah
509.829.6235; silverlakewinery.com

Yakima Greenway
111 S. 18th Street, Yakima
509.453.8280; yakimagreenway.org

**Above: Teepees illuminate
the night at Cherry Wood Bed,
Breakfast & Barn in Zillah, Wash.**

Photo by Julie Austin

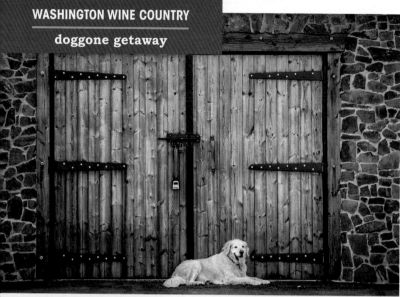

Cave B Inn

NESTLED UPON A CLIFFSIDE OVERLOOKING THE GORGE, SITS CAVE B INN & SPA RESORT.

Located in the heart of wine country, with the Gorge Amphitheater on one side and panoramic views on the other, **Cave B Inn & Spa Resort** is one of our all-time favorite places to visit with our pooch. In fact, this is our second visit to Cave B, but the first since they added yurts to their repetoire—dog-friendly yurts!

STAY On our last visit, we stayed in one of the resort's gorgeous and dog friendly **Cliffehouses**, which feature floor to ceiling windows, separate seating area and bedroom, with a two-sided gas fireplace in between, high curved ceilings and wood floors, soaking tub and separate Italian granite shower, luxurious king-size bed, and French doors that open to an outdoor patio area, where you can enjoy the spectacular sunset over the Columbia River. Pure heaven, especially with a glass of Caveman Red in your hand and a hound by your side.

Equally divine, but a bit more rustic, are the resort's dog-friendly **Desert Yurts**. There are 25 yurts in all, perched on a hillside overlooking the property with sweeping views of the Gorge and surrounding vineyard. And, just because they are more rustic than say, a Cliffehouse, it doesn't mean you have to sacrifice comfort.

Photos by Julie Clegg

Clockwise from top: The "Cave" at Cave B Inn; enjoy an amazing meal at Tendrils; one of Cave B's signature wines, Caveman Red; sip wine and enjoy the view; the dog-friendly Desert Yurts. Next page: Take a stroll through the vineyard to the main Inn.

GETTING HERE Follow I-90 E and I-82 E/US-97 S to Yakima. Take exit 31A-31B from I-82 E/US-97 S. Continue onto N 1st St to downtown Yakima.

Photo by Julie Clegg

ach yurt features a private bathroom, with walk-in shower, sofa, table nd chairs, mini-fridge, teapot, and Ipod docking station. The décor minimalist, but hey, it's a yurt. Really, all the décor you need is the ool skydome, perfect for stargazing while relaxing with Rover in the omfort of your king sized bed.

Once you drop off your gear at the yurts, venture over to Cave B's **asting Room** to sample the inn's amazing range of varietals, all grown the estate. It's hard to choose from the 20-plus wines available, but e recommend starting with a 2015 Harvest Semillon, followed by our vorite, a 2017 Sauvignon Blanc. Next, try the 2018 Dry Rosé, followed y another one of our favorites, a 2015 Barbera. The deliciousness ntinues with a 2015 Tempranillo and the amazing 2015 XXX Cabernet auvignon. Yum! While the Tasting Room itself is not dog friendly, ur pooch is welcome on the patio, where you can kick back, sip vard-winning wine and enjoy the view. Life is good.

T But, life is about to get even better. Following your tasting, it's me to head to **Tendrils**, Cave B's gourmet restaurant. Start your meal ith a Roasted Baby Beet Salad, with roasted beets, wild baby arugula, erbed goat cheese, extra virgin olive oil, and balsamic reduction. ext of course, is your appetizer and we recommend the Frito Misto, mprised of calamari, prawns, Walla Walla sweet onions, and lemon heels dusted with house breading ad served with lemon smoked aprika sauce. And, now for the coup de grâce—dry aged, grass fed eef tenderloin, served with roasted garlic and thyme mashed po-

tatoes, green beans, roasted cipollini onions, and your choice of Caveman Red demi-glaze, Reyes blue cheese cream, or a compound butter sauce. Wow! Of course, no meal is complete without dessert, so we suggest you try a few! Start with the Berry Crème Brûlée, made with vanilla custard and seasonal berries, topped with a hard sugar shell. Or, try the Chocolate Lava Cake, with a, ooey, gooey melted chocolate center. Or, how about the J.P. Trodden bourbon and bread pudding, topped with vanilla ice cream and bourbon caramel?

Clearly, the menu at Tendril's is amazing, and it's worth noting that a wide variety of organic fruits, vegetables and herbs are grown in the Chef's Garden, located near Cave B's main Inn, and used in many of the dishes.

Post-dinner, take the 10 minute walk back to your yurt and be sure to look up at the night sky blanketed in stars—you might even see the Milky Way!

Enjoy sweeping views of the Columbia River Gorge.

After a relaxing morning at the yurt, head back to Tendrils for brunch, this time to enjoy the expansive outdoor patio, where dogs are welcome. Brunch includes the option of building your own omelet, with a choice of ham, bacon, sausage, spinach, tomatoes, mushroom, onions, peppers, cheddar, swiss and/or goat cheese. Pair that with a mimosa and...yum!

PLAY Following brunch, the next order of business is to work off some calories with a hike on the **Columbia River Trail**. Taking you off the plateau and down into the gorge, the trail consists of both flat and moderately steep terrain along a marked trail. As the trail finishes its western descent to the gorge floor, it opens to the Columbia River, where you will find a rocky beach, with Bird Island just to the South—a popular landing area for migrating birds. For a longer hike, take the Waterfall Loop Trail, which takes you even deeper into the gorge to Fitzpatrick Waterfall. Combined with the Columbia River Trail, the hike takes about three hours, so bring plenty of water to keep you and your canine companion hydrated.

Back at the resort, a post-hike visit to the **Spa at Cave B Inn** is a must. The Spa offers a wide range of services including Swedish, hot stone and deep tissue massage plus facials and body treatments that include a lavender sea salt exfoliation wrap.

Another feature of Cave B Inn's (among its many), is its proximity to the Gorge Amphitheater—right next door, as a matter of fact! As

you probably know, between May and October, the Gorge hosts a star-studded lineup of performers. However, book early, because—not surprisingly, Cave B sells out. For a schedule of concerts at the Gorge, visit livenation.com.

Whether you visit for a concert, or simply to get away from the city (it's only a 2.5 hour drive from Seattle), Cave B Inn Spa & Resort will not disappoint, especially while in the company of your dog. The food is amazing, the wine is divine, the yurts are comfy and cozy, the scenery is spectacular—and most importantly, your canine travel companion is treated like the VIP he is—a Very Important Pet, that is! 🐾

MORE INFORMATION
Cave B Inn Spa & Resort
344 Silica Road, NW, Quincy
888.785.2283; cavebinn.com

Northwest Yurts

UP YOUR CAMPING GAME AND BOOK A DOG-FRIENDLY YURT FOR YOU AND ROVER.

you have never gone camping in a yurt, you will be pleasantly surprised at how much is like camping in a tent, yet, with conveniences of a cabin, uch as electricity and heat, and futon bed. What's even better now there are yurts that allow ou to take your dog with you. Here are a few in Washington nd Oregon to get you started.

One of the dog-friendly yurts at Cave B Inn.

Photo by Julie Clegg

WASHINGTON If you and your dog enjoy bird watching r simply walking along the beach, then **Grayland Beach tate Park** in Grayland, Wash. is the place to visit. There is 412-acre park with "marine camping" on the oceanfront n Southwest Washington. They have four pet-friendly urts available and are open year-round.

Near Mount St. Helens is **Sequest State Park**. With 75-acres of forest and shoreline on Silver Lake. There s one pet-friendly yurt in the park, and within walking istance of the Mount St. Helens Visitor Center.

A little further inland is the **Kanaskat-Plamer State ark**. Situated on a 320-acre park along the Green River Gorge. You can enjoy trout fishing and picnics along he shoreline. River rafting and kayaking is only for the xpert-enthusiast. They have one pet-friendly yurt available, open year-round.

Washington parks require that you plan at least one day head if you want to make a reservation or as early as nine months before your arrival. And, there is a $15 per night ee for pets. They do not have a limit to the number of pets r size. To make reservations, go online at parks.wa.gov or all 888.226.7688.

OREGON If you want to enjoy some coastal seafood while you're camping with your dog, **Umpqua Lighthouse State Park** is going to be your paradise located in Reedsport,

Ore. They offer "some of the best crabbing and sports fishing along the Oregon coast." They have one pet-friendly yurt and are open year-round.

Beverly Beach State Park in Newport, Ore. has some campsites along the beach. The main campground is along a creek and "… is one of the state's largest." This campground has two pet-friendly yurts and is open year-round.

William M. Tugman State Park located off highway 101 near Lakeside, Ore. is located on Eel Lake and is perfect for boat fishing or sitting on the edge of the dock. There are also trails through wooded forests where you might have the opportunity to see wildlife such as deer, osprey and eagles. There are six pet-friendly yurts available year-round.

All Oregon parks require that you plan at least one day ahead if you want to make a reservation or as early as nine months before your arrival. Prices include a $10 fee per night pet fee with a limit of two dogs per site. There are no size limitations.

For reservations, call 800.452.5687 or you can reserve online at OregonStateParks.org. Unfortunately, online reservations are not available if you plan to take your pet with you. 🐾

WASHINGTON WINE COUNTRY

Washington's Yakima Valley is one of the oldest wine regions in the state, growing and producing approximately a third of the state's wine. This region is celebrated for its chardonnay, merlot, cabernet sauvignon and of course, dog-friendly wineries. Here at CityDog Magazine, we love wine and we love dogs, so we've compiled a list of some of the Yakima Valley's wineries that welcome your canine companions. *Pictured above: Cooper at Wilrigdge Vineyard.*

Airfield Estates Winery (*airfieldwines.com*)
560 Merlot Drive, Prosser
Located in the heart of the Yakima Valley, Airfield Estates happily welcomes leashed, well-behaved and well-socialized dogs. to hang out in the tasting room, on the patio and elsewhere on the grounds.

Apex Cellars (*apexwinecellars.com*)
357 Port Street, Prosser
This winery is celebrated for making whites and reds that are equally amazing. The team at Apex Cellars greets leashed pups inside the facility with a treat and water dish—just keep it classy by scooping your dog's poop.

Bonair Winery (*bonairwine.com*)
500 South Bonair Road, Zillah
Owners of Bonair, Gail and Shirley Puryea, welcome four-legged friends at their winery. The property boasts a large, grassy area, so grab a glass or two from the tasting room and enjoy a picnic on the lawn.

Cultura Wine (*culturawine.com*)
601 Highland Drive, Zillah
Known for its Bordeaux style reds, Cultura likes to think of itself as a pit stop for wine tasters and dogs to rest and refuel. The only request? Dogs must remain on leash while on the property.

amache Vinters (*gamachevintners.com*)
5 Cabernet Ct., Prosser

ounded in 1982, Gamache Vinters knows Washington
ine from lush and well-balanced reds to refreshing
hites, including special wines from its heritage and
rary collections. A very dog-friendly place, sip on Old
orld style wines while your pup snacks on dog treats.

aryhill Winery (*maryhillwinery.com*)
74 Highway 14, Goldendale

aryhill is a robust winery with a tasting room, reserve
om and vine-covered outdoor terrace. Leashed, well-
annered dogs are welcome anywhere on the property
lcuding the nearby bocce ball court.

aradisos Del Sol (*paradisosdelsol.com*)
30 Highland Drive, Zillah

aradisos Del Sol makes it easy for dog owners to enjoy
ine tasting with a line outside that Fido can be clipped
while humans head into the tasting room. The win-
y provides water at all times along with facilities for
cnicking and space for dogs to romp.

eeping Dog Wines (*sleepingdogwines.com*)
804 N Whitmore PR NW, Benton City

ptly named, Sleeping Dog is home to Jet, the ca-
ne "valet," who greets friendly mutts that visit this
g-loving winery. Sleeping Dog's website shares,
hroughout this journey, there has been a canine
sociate providing amusement, companionship and
versight…Besides, we happen to like dogs and the
me just seemed to work!"

eppe Cellars (*facebook.com/SteppeCellars*)
91 Chaffee Road, Sunnyside

eppe Cellars is a family run winery made up of
cond-generation farmers. Dogs can often be spotted
leash in the picnic area and running off leash in the
erry orchard next door to the winery.

wo Mountain Winery (*twomountainwinery.com*)
51 Cheyne Road, Zillah

wo Mountain produces everything from Rosé to Syrah
ith the help of resident winery dogs. Canine compan-
ns are invited to run, play and dig in the orchard or
y in the grass, but they must be on leash once inside.

MORE DOG-FRIENDLY WASHINGTON WINERIES

- ▶ Agate Field Vineyard (*agatefield.com*)
- ▶ Alexandria Nicole (*alexandrianicolecellars.com*)
- ▶ AntoLin Cellars (*antolincellars.com*)
- ▶ Barrel Springs Winery (*barrelspringswinery.com*)
- ▶ Chandler Reach Vineyards (*chandlerreach.com*)
- ▶ Cooper Wine Company (*cooperwinecompany.com*)
- ▶ Covet Cellars (*covetwine.com*)
- ▶ Daven Lore Winery (*davenlore.com*)
- ▶ Dineen Vineyards (*dineenvineyards.com*)
- ▶ Domanico Cellars (*domanicocellars.com*)
- ▶ Gilbert Cellars (*gilbertcellars.com*)
- ▶ Hogue Cellars (*hoguecellars.com*)
- ▶ Hyatt Vineyards (*hyattvineyards.net*)
- ▶ J Bell Cellars and Lavender (*jbellcellars.com*)
- ▶ Kana Winery (*kanawinery.com*)
- ▶ Knight Hill Winery (*knighthillwine.com*)
- ▶ Maison de Padgett (*maisondepadgettwinery.com*)
- ▶ Martinez Winery (*martinezwine.com*)
- ▶ Mas Chappell Winery (*maschappellwinery.com*)
- ▶ Mercer Wine Estates (*mercerwine.com*)
- ▶ Milbrandt Vineyards (*milbrandtvineyards.com*)
- ▶ Owen Roe (*owenroe.com*)
- ▶ Pontin Del Roza Winery (*pontindelroza.com*)
- ▶ Portteus Winery (*portteus.com*)
- ▶ Purple Star Wines (*purplestarwines.com*)
- ▶ Rider Cellars (*ridercellars.com*)
- ▶ Severino Cellars (*severinocellars.com*)
- ▶ Silver Lake Winery (*silverlakewinery.com*)
- ▶ Tanjuli Winery (*tanjuli.com*)
- ▶ Tapteil Vineyard (*tapteil.com*)
- ▶ Wilridge (*wilridgewinery.com*)
- ▶ Thurston-Wolfe Winery (*thurstonwolfe.com*)
- ▶ Treveri Cellars (*trevericellars.com*)
- ▶ Tucannon Cellars (*tucannoncellars.com*)

South Central Washington

Bordering the beautiful Columbia River Gorge, South Central Washington is rich in stunning scenery, quaint towns, and delicious wine (yes, wine).

oto by Emily Rieman

SPOKANE & GOLDENDALE, WASHINGTON

VANCOUVER LOCATION OPENING EARLY 2019

DOG FRIENDLY YEAR-ROUND

SHOWCASING THE RICH AND DIVERSE FLAVORS OF WASHINGTON STATE WINE WITH PASSION. PATIENCE. BALANCE.

"Pacific Northwest Winery of the Year"

@MARYHILLWINERY
MARYHILLWINERY.COM

Maryhill
WINERY

THE COLUMBIA RIVER GORGE IS A DESIGNATED NATIONAL SCENIC AREA — AND FOR GOOD REASON. WITH AWE-INSPIRING WATERFALLS, SURROUNDING MOUNTAINS, AND SPECTACULAR SCENERY AT EVERY TURN, IT'S A TRIP YOU WON'T SOON FORGET.

ocated 45 minutes from Portland, and about four hours from eattle, is the mighty Columbia River Gorge. The Columbia River car-es water from the mountains of British Columbia, Canada down to erge with the pristine waters of the Cascade Mountains of Washing-n state, where it tumbles through the gorge, or canyon, where the ver separates the states of Oregon and Washington, to eventually mpty out into the Pacific Ocean. The gorge portion of the river reach-s heights of approximately 4,000 feet and is roughly 80 miles long. ruly it is awe inspiring, so much so that it hold federally protected atus as a national scenic area.

The Columbia River Gorge has massive formations of columnar asalt, and is a perfect recreational area. Hood River, Oregon is a ecca for kiteboarders and windsurfers as the blasts of wind that come rough the gorge are perfect for these activities.

Stop in for a bite to eat at **Solstice**, with a dog-friendly patio and rganic pizza, it's a perfect place to sit and watch all the river activity. beer is more to your liking, check out **Double Mountain Brewery** hich is also dog friendly

For a better understanding of the area, visit the Columbia Gorge Interpre-tive center just outside of Stevenson, Wash. The Center highlights the history of the Columbia Gorge, recording the amazing stories of endurance and change of the canyon. Another must see is **Multnomah Falls**. 620 feet tall, the Falls are two-tiered and is the tallest waterfall in the state of Oregon.

Up and down the gorge, there are spots for bird watching, fishing, paddle boarding, and boating, and the land that hugs the river is perfect for hiking and mountain biking. With a few sup-plies for you and Fido, you simply can-not go wrong with a visit to this area.

Photo courtesy of Skamania Lodge

Above: An aerial view of Skamania Lodge in Stevenson, Wash.

Photos by Emily Rieman

Clockwise from top: Thya relaxes in the comfortable lobby area at Skamania Lodge; the lodge's restaurant features a stunning view; the lobby at Skamania; an aerial view of Skamania Lodge and Columbia River; River Rock Lounge's delicious seafood salad.

GETTING HERE Take I-5 S to I-205 S then east on SR-14. At Stevenson, turn left on Rock Creek Drive and left onto Skamania Lodge Way.

South Central Washington

VISIT THE COLUMBIA RIVER GORGE IN ALL ITS GLORY, WITH YOUR FOUR LEGGED FRIEND IN ALL OF THEIRS

Skamania Lodge in Stevenson, Washington is an ideal destination for dog lovers. The 175-acre wooded estate offers guests, two- and four-legged alike, a glimpse into one of the nation's most beautiful natural wonders, while providing all of the creature comforts a human and canine could want. Opening its doors in 1993, Skamania was designed to mirror the glory of the great lodges of the early 1900s.

STAY When you arrive at Skamania Lodge the Columbia River Gorge comes alive in all its glory. With towering old-growth timbers, the Lodge has a warm and inviting lobby area. You'll stop and stare at the huge, 85 foot tall fireplace, surrounded by comfy leather chairs and walls of windows that overlook the splendor of the river and the acreage of the Lodge. Select a glass of wine from the guest welcome table and make yourself at home in one of the large chairs while you and your best fuzzy buddy relax as you are checking in to Skamania.

It will be hard to leave the grand lobby of the Lodge, but once you get to your dog-friendly room, you will be glad you worked up the self-control. Skamania Lodge caters to dogs. When making your reservation mention that your pup will accompany you and get ready to be surprised. When you open

bove: Thya takes full advantage of Skamania Lodge's dog-friendly
plicy. Right: Be sure to take a detour to beautiful Multnomah Falls.

e door to your room your dog will find a welcome packet loaded with
podies including a treat, toy, leash, and towel for wiping down muddy
ws. But the luxury is not limited to your dog, it also extends to the
vo-legged kind. Depending on where you've been located, your room
ill have views of the Cascade Mountains, the Columbia River Gorge
rests, the river itself, or the resort grounds. Whatever view you get, rest-
ssured it will be breathtaking. Each of the Lodge's rooms are expansive,
ppointed with Pacific Northwest artwork, a king size bed, cozy gas
replace, television, WiFi and high speed internet, robes, hair dryer,
ning board, coffee maker, mini refrigerator, and windows that open
let in the fresh air. Tip: Ask for a room on the first floor with a patio to
low your dog easy access for potty breaks.

AY After you have unpacked, set up your dog's space, and retrieved a
ater bottle, it's time to explore the grounds. Set out on the 1.7-mile **Lake**
op Trail that winds through the woods past Wy'East Lake and Lilly Pad
ke and keep an eye out for wildlife including birds, frogs, turtles and
er. Join up with the 1.5-mile **Creek Loop Trail** that leads to a spectacular
ewpoint that overlooks the Columbia River and Benson Plateau. If you
ek a more challenging hike, the **Gorge Loop Trail** leads into a canyon,
ith switchbacks on the way back up to the Lodge, and features views of
e Columbia River and Bridge of the Gods, a steel truss cantilever-styled
idge that spans the entire river, connecting Oregon to Washington state.

T If all of the hiking has worked up your appetites, then it's time to go
ck to your room for a brief clean up and attend to your pup's needs
fore heading to the **River Rock Lounge** for a meal. We recommend

the Lounge for it's casual, lighter
fare menu that focuses on small
plates with a local twist such as
Skamania mac 'n' cheese, Columbia
Gorge pizza, and stealhead tacos.
The grilled petite shoulder steak
and roasted garlic and red pepper
hummus with grilled pita, tomato,
cucumber, olives, and sun-dried
tomato tapenade are favorites. Try
a regional craft beer, a delicious
signature cocktail, or even
champagne by the glass—the River
Rock Lounge aims to please.

The Skamania Lodge has other
dining options including the **Cascade**
Dining Room, where executive chef
Matt Hale sources nearly all of
his epicurean offerings within 50
miles of the lodge including seared

Photos by Emily Rieman

plays magically, shimmering off the rocks and water, appearing to wink at you and your pup as you stroll by. The evening light changes with each minute on the banks of the Columbia River Gorge, and makes for a wonderful time to capture some photographs to share with your friends and family. When you're ready to snuggle in bed, or take a nice warm bubble bath, return to your room, wipe down your pup's paws and settle in the for the evening because tomorrow w have a lot in store for you.

Waking rested, and after grabbing a bite to eat and taking care of your dog's requirements it's time to put a little excitement in your life and try a few things the Lodge has to offer like biking an golfing. Not enough excitement for you? How does whitewater rafting, ziplining, or visiting the aerial park to scale across wind-driven bridges and tight-wires.

If you are more of the massage loving type, then the **Waterleaf Spa** will rejuvenate your mind, body, and soul. There are over 45 different recreational choices available to you at Skamania Lodge, and the property's trail system offers miles of hiking paths, with magnificent views of the Columbia River Gorge and Cascade Mountains. We recommend that you and Fido drive in Stevenson and hike the six mile **Dog Mountain Trail**, along the

salmon with roasted asparagus and cranberry apricot compote, smoked duck breast with braised red cabbage and huckleberry sauce, and bone-in ribeye with house made Yukon Gold fries and demi-herb butter.

From April through September, the outdoor **Greenside Grille** offers golfers, and those exploring the nature trails, casual fare including sandwiches, wraps, BLTs, hamburgers, and hotdogs. The Lodge also offers their signature dishes all packaged to go for in room or picnic-style so you and your pup can enjoy dinner on the grounds.

PLAY After dinner is a good time for an evening stroll with the pup. The Lodge requires that you keep your dog on a six-foot leash, the size left in the pet welcome packet, and offers potty pick up bags throughout the resort. Walking the grounds at sunset while looking out at the Columbia River Gorge is something you'll remember for a long time. The golden amber light of the setting sun

Top: The views at Skamania Lodge are stunning. Left: Enjoy a glass of award-winning wine at Maryhill Winery.

wis & Clark Highway, ith a one mile loop at e summit for an excelnt view of the Columa River Gorge.

Whatever you decide r your morning exerse, you can't miss stopng at **Maryhill Winery** Goldendale, Wash. pproximately an hour rtheast of Skamania dge on highway 97. cated in the Columbia orge wine region on bluff overlooking the olumbia River, with ectacular views of Mt. ood, this destination winery is defitely one of the more breathtaking ineries you may have seen to date, nd best of all, it's dog friendly. If ur timing is fortunate, you and ur pup may get to go on a behindne-scenes tour of the winery to see here the award-winning wines e made. Maryhill produces over) varieties of wine, from cabernet chardonnay, merlot to malbec, nd is home to a 3,000 square-foot sting room, a 1,200 square-foot eserve room with private courtard, four bocce ball courts, and a ine-covered, Tuscan-style outdoor rrace, all of which are family and og friendly.

End your tour on the terrace, nd treat yourself to a flight of elicious red and white wines ncluding a Zinfandel that's quite xquisite. After your tasting, you'll nderstand why Maryhill has been ecognized as Winery of the Year y San Francisco International Wine ompetition, Winemaker of the ear by Indy International Wine

Photo by Emily Rieman

Enjoy the stunning views from the terrace at Maryhill Winery, the place to be for dog lovers and wine lovers alike.

Competition, Washington Winery of the Year by Wine Press Northwest and Best Destination Winery by Seattle Magazine. Pick up a few bottles to give to your loved ones as gifts, or for yourself to enjoy when you get back home.

If you're staying another night, and looking for a more casual place to stay, the family owned and operated **Ponderosa Motel** is located minutes away from Maryhill at the foothills of the beautiful Simcoe Mountains. The rooms are spacious and clean, with a coffee maker, microwave, small refrigerator, and television with Direct TV. Keeping with the casual theme, grab a burger and a beer for dinner at the **Top Hat** and eggs benedict for breakfast at the **Town House Café**, both located in downtown Goldendale.

Pat your pup on the head, because life doesn't get much better than a trip to the breathtaking Columbia River Gorge. 🐾

MORE INFORMATION

Skamania Lodge
1131 SW Skamania Lodge Way
Stevenson, Washington
509.427.7700; skamania.com

Maryhill Winery
9774 Hwy 14, Goldendale
877.MARYHILL
maryhillwinery.com

Ponderosa Motel
775 East Broadway, Goldendale
509.773.5842
ponderosamotelgoldendale.com

Top Hat
124 W Main Street, Goldendale
509.773.9968
facebook.com/The-Top-Hat

Town House Café
114 W Allyn Street, Goldendale
509.773.2210
facebook.com/Townhousecafe

Portland & Oregon

From the city of Portland to the Oregon Coast, this Pacific wonderland offers dreamers and dog lovers alike a place to explore off the beaten path.

Photo by Julie Clegg

The Destination for Dogs...

Dogs Allowed Cannon Beach is The Destination for Dogs and for the owner who is looking for a little something more.

DOGS ALLOWED
CANNON BEACH

148-B Hemlock St • (503) 440-8740
dogsallowedcannonbeach.com

Sit! Stay
PET PHOTOGRAPHY

AWESOME PORTRAITS OF YOUR FAVORITE FURRY FRIENDS!

Lifestyle pet photography, in Portland and beyond

 Get to know us on Instagram! – instagram.com/portlandpetphotographer

lindsay@sitstaypetphotography.com   (503) 901-3026   www.sitstaypetphotography.com

YOU KNOW WHAT MAKES OREGON'S 363 MILES OF PUBLIC COASTLINE, GREEN FORESTS AND SPARKLING MOUNTAIN LAKES EVEN BETTER? GETTING TO TAKE YOUR BEST FRIEND ALONG WITH YOU.

Oregon is a dog lover's dream, from the city of Portland, with over 30 dog parks, to the state's pristine beaches, where dogs are allowed to run leash free. Whether you live here, or just visiting, the places to sit, stay and play with your pooch are seemingly endless. We've traveled the coast with our canine companions, sipped wine with our four-legged friends, hiked Mt. Hood with our hounds, and explored the neighborhoods of Portland to dig up the best these places have to offer.

Oregon is known for its diverse landscape of forests, mountains, farms and beaches. The city of Portland is famed for its quirky, avant-garde culture and is home to iconic coffee shops, boutiques, farm-to-table restaurants and microbreweries. The coast features 363 miles of stunning public coastline dotted with lighthouses, fishing villages and dramatic scenery. Oregon's wine country, the Willamette Valley is home to more than 500 wineries, many of them dog friendly.

It's no wonder Oregon is a favorite among dog lovers!

Above: The Oregon Coast's world-famous Haystack Rock. Wine tasting in the Willamette Valley is a must-do with your dog.

Left photo by Lindsay Bacca; above photo by Julie Clegg

Portland

PORTLAND IS HAPPENING NOW AND IT'S ESPECIALLY HAPPENING FOR POOCHES.

Portland is happening now. That'the tagline at the Travel Portland website (*travelportland.com*). Even better, Portland is happening for pooches and it's happening at **Lucky Labrador Brewing Company.** Celebrating 20 years in business and three dog-friendly brew pubs, the Lucky Lab is top dog on the Portland pooch scene. Pop-in to their flagship location on Hawthorne for a bite to eat and a pint to drink. To say the Lucky Lab is laid back would be an understatement, which makes it perfect for dog lovers. There's nothing fancy or fussy here—just a laid-back, casual environment, with simple sandwiches and tasty brews plus a heated, outdoor patio area to enjoy your refreshments with Rover.

SIT Another option for beer and dog lovers alike is **Base Camp Brewing Company.** Open seven days a week, Base Camp's taproom and dog-friendly patio is the perfect spot to enjoy a good beer and a bite to eat from one of their food cart partners, **KOi Fusion**, serving up a funky fusion of Korean BBQ and fresh Mexican flavors or **Gonzo Falafel and Hummus**, featuring delicious vegetarian and vegan fare.

Speaking of food carts, Portland is a Mecca of mobile eateries, serving hungry patrons everything from Russian pierogies to Japanese ramen to good ol' southern barbecue. But, don't just take our word for

Clockwise from top: Taking a time out to enjoy the view at Vera Katz Eastbank Esplanade; the dog-friendly outdoor patio at Lucky Labrador Brewing Company; a Portland icon, the White Stag sign greets drivers on the Burnside Bridge; enjoying a walk at Tryon Creek State Park, located just 15 minutes from downtown Portland.

To commence drooling, just visit foodcartsportland.com, an ode to Portland's food cart culture, and a practical guide for where to find them and what to eat once you get there, including **Tidbit Food Farm Garden**, one of the more welcoming and dog-friendly food cart lots in the city, with vendors setup to surround a cozy seating area complete with a fireplace.

While the choices for food cart eats are seemingly endless, a trip to Portland would not be complete without a visit to the **Tin Shed Garden Café**. Located in the Alberta Arts District, and enthusiastically dog-friendly, this funky little shack is notable for its rib-

This dog could not be more chill, hanging out at Mississippi Records.

tickling fare. Menu items for people include "Fetch," a bacon and egg scramble covered with sharp cheddar, tomato and green onion, "Good Dog," which features pork sausage, jalapeño, bell pepper, onion and egg scramble, smothered with Tillamook cheddar, salsa fresca and chipotle aioli, and "Roll Over," a sausage and egg scramble smothered with apple wood smoked bacon gravy. Each is served over potato cakes or cheese grits. And, that's just for breakfast!

The dinner menu is just as ridiculous (in a good way), for dogs and humans, with items like "Mac-of-the-Day" and "Fungus Amongus," with sauteed portabella mushrooms and carmelized onions, topped with avocado, chipotle aioli and pepper jack cheese on toasted sourdough bread. Dogs enjoy their own menu, with a choice of chicken, ground beef or pork mixed with rice and sweet potatoes. And, dinner would not be complete without dessert—just try and resist a slice of chocolate cake layered with raspberry jam and peanut butter mousse, while your pooch enjoys a dish of peanut butter-banana ice cream.

The cozy garden seating has an outdoor fireplace and is the perfect spot to hang with your pup and every Tuesday night is Dog Lovers Night. For every regularly priced people item, you receive one doggie menu item for free. And, speaking of doggie love, the Tin Shed has teamed up with Portland non-profits like Oregon Humane and Fences for Fido. When you purchase a Tin Shed doggie bandana for $8, all of the proceeds go to the one of these organizations. Then, anytime your dog comes to the Tin Shed wearing its bandana, he gets 50% off his doggie dinner.

Next, explore Portland's posh and polished Pearl District—a testament to the city's smart urban planning, where **Lovejoy Bakers** rises to the level of a hidden neighborhood gem. Known for its bread and delightful desserts, Lovejoy also offers a full breakfast and lunch menu, and most recently dinner.

PLAY Work off some of those calories acquired over the last couple of day with a hike at **Tryon Creek State Park**. Located about 15 minutes from downtown Portland, Tryon is Oregon's only state park within a major metropolitan area.

With 670 acres of forest and a 2.7 mile loop trail, it's perfect for an afternoon hike with your pooch— but, because it's a state park, dogs must remain on leash.

For off-leash fun, Portland is the place, with over 30 off-leash areas—

Photo courtesy of Travel Portland

Coordinate your visit to coincide with their happy hour, Monday through Friday from 5-7 p.m. You ca enjoy snacks and wine whil your dog plays or luxuriate in his spa service. Sniff Dog bright, open-spaced store sells food, toys, beds, and lo cal, handmade dog cookies.

Another store worth you visit is Hip Hound, located at the corner of NW 23rd and Burnside Street. Hip Hound is the place to go fo everything from treats, foo bowls, and toys to outerwea and accessories. After some shopping, relax in the store aptly-named Java Hound Coffee Bar to enjoy a hot m cha and lavender shortbrea cookie while your pup laps up a puppuccino (whipped goat's milk with cookie nibbles floating on top).

Another favorite, be sure to swing by **Green Dog Pet Supply**, located in northeast Portland, where they carry hundreds of locally-made products including one of our favorites, **Cycle Dog** (collars and leashes made in Portland with recycled bicycle inner tubes).

Clockwise from above: The Tasting Bar at Southeast Wine Collective; Portland, a.k.a. City of Roses, is home to a number of ecletic neighboroods; Green Dog Pet Supply is stocked with healthy food.

from fenced dog parks that are leash-free during park hours to unfenced areas that are open to off-leash dogs during designated hours. Opt for **Chimney Park**, a full-time, 16-acre dog park, located just four miles from downtown. For a complete list of Portland's off-leash areas (fenced and unfenced), see the following pages.

If you want to skip the off-leash thing altogether but let your dog enjoy some indoor playtime, check out **Sniff Dog Hotel**, where they can also enjoy a hot bath and some spa treatments. If group play is not your dog's style, then he can have a personalized walk on the rooftop track. Maybe your dog prefers to take some R&R on his own in which case you can reserve a private day-stay where he'll have his own room and a Sniff Dog staff person who will take him on personalized outings.

STAY Portland has several pet-friendly place to stay and one of our favorites is **Hotel Rose**, with its wildly colorful interiors and eclecti furnishings. The rooms are large, bright, and have all the modern amenities you

ed for a comfortable
ay, like flat-screen TVs
d Keurig coffeemak-
s. The bathrooms are
odern and spacious, with
n oversized shower and
infall showerhead as well
amenities like Tommy
ahama bath products
d a plush bathrobe and
atching slippers, no
ss. The beds are super
mfy—for you and your
ooch. As part of the
neapple Pup Package,
ur-legged guests get their
wn dog bed plus a water
owl, treats, and baggy
spenser. And, speaking
baggies, Hotel Rose
located directly across
om **Tom McCall Water-
ont Park** on the Willa-
ette River, making potty
reaks convenient and
enic. If you're an early
ser, ready to explore what
eeps Portland weird, grab
our caffeine fix and a
uick bite at the Pineapple
spresso bar on your way
ut the door. Or, if you
refer to stay in bed all day
no judgment), the in-room
enu has delicious options
or breakfast, lunch and
inner. If you would rather
t down for a full meal,
ottle + Kitchen serves up
lobally-inspired, locally-
efined comfort food and
raft cocktails.

TAY At the the equally
og-friendly **Sentinel Ho-**

**Clockwise from top: Coffee, pastries and canines at Lovejoy Bakery; taking a
break at Portland's luxurious Sentinel Hotel; latte art at Lovejoy Bakery.**

tel, the mantra is "Make It So." What does this mean? It means, when you stay at the
iconic, luxury hotel, located in the heart of downtown Portland, you are completely
catered to, whether it's a basic amenity or a whimsical fancy—and, the same goes for
your canine companion.

For starters, Fido has his own room service menu. With items like Brats-n-Tots
(savory beef sausage links, sweet potatoes and Granny Smith apples) and Wingaling
(brown rice and chicken wings simmered in gravy), your dog will be drooling in no
time—and, at just $7.95 each, these doggie culinary delights won't break the bank.
Of course, you also have your own room service menu, and with items like filet
mignon, with mashed potatoes and cabernet mushroom sauce or dungeness crab,
shrimp and brie stuffed salmon, you'll be drooling, too! If you prefer to venture out,
you don't have to go far to find fine dining. **Jake's Grill**, located on the first floor of
the hotel's East Wing, is an essential fixture on the downtown Portland dining scene.

Top: Travel Portland; bottom two: Emily Rieman

Portland, Oregon • 175

Clockwise from top: Cool wall art at the Jupiter Hotel; the dog-friendly suite at Hotel Rose; grab a cocktail at Bottle + Kitchen.

Photos by Lindsay Bacca

When it comes to pampering your pooch, the Sentinel spares nothing. Rover will be greeted with a comfy bed, food and water bowls, a cute toy, tasty treats and a list of local pet resources, from dog walkers to pet psychics and everything in between.

Remember the "Make It So" mantra we mention above? Well, there's an actual "Make It So" button on your in-room phone. Does your furry friend suffer from sore muscles, arthritis, or depression? Push the "Make It So" button and help is just a phone call away. In-room acupuncture, massage and Reiki, as well as a phone psychic reading can be arranged. Does your four-legged pal deserve a "spaw" day? Sentinel staff is happy to arrange a grooming ap-

pointment at **Noah's Arf** or **D'tai** in the Pearl District. Looking for that perfect gift or a tasty treat for your best friend? Sentinel guests receive 10% off at **Urban Fauna**. Also, doggie daycare at **Virginia Woof** or dog walking services by **Lexi Dog** can be arranged if business takes you away for the day.

While your canine's every need is catered to, have no worries — yours are catered to, too. In addition to the pillow, iPod and spiritual menus, there is also an ice cream menu. With flavors like Sea Salt with Caramel Ribbon, Honey Balsamic Strawberry with Cracked Pepper, Almond Brittle with Salted Ganache, and Pear and Blue Cheese, order a pint from Portland's favorite ice cream, **Salt & Straw**, and your sweet tooth will be satisfied.

STAY Once a mid-century motor lodge, the completely renovated **Jupiter Hotel** has been transformed into a beautiful — and dog-friendly — boutique hotel. Located in one of Portland's hippest neighborhoods, the cultural Eastside, boasts more than 60 of the top bars, eateries, breweries and shops nearby.

The Jupiter offers a variety of rooms to fit your needs and your budget. The Deuce features two pillow-top queen beds and down comforters, a 32" flat screen TV, modern Tomita Design desks, eco-friendly amenities, and free wireless internet.

Outside the room is a lovely courtyard, with ample seating and sparkly chandelier lighting, surrounded by lush bamboo. Grab a

e pet-friendly Hotel Rose provides a cushy dog bed for your pooch.

p of organic, locally-roasted coffee from the lobby (it's complimentary) and lax with your four-legged friend—you'll be amazed at how easy is it to strike a conversation with fellow Jupiter guests.

If it's time to start thinking food, **Doug Fir Lounge** is located right xt door and while it's not dog friendly, you can order room service. The eakfast, lunch and dinner options are amazing, with items like the Portland angover, Garden Benedict and a classic Patty Melt. Yum!

Wth all that there is to discover, there is no doubt Portland has earned its rank-g as one of the pooch friendliest cities in the country. To learn more about where sit, stay and play in Portland, visit travelportland.com. 🐾

ORE INFORMATION

cky Lab Brew Pub on Hawthorne
5 S.E. Hawthorne Boulevard
3.236.3555; luckylab.com/hawthorne-brew-pub

cky Lab Beer Hall on Quimby
45 NW Quimby Street
3-517-4352; luckylab.com/quimby-beer-hall

cky Lab Public House at Multnomah Village
75 SW Capitol Highway
3-244-2537; luckylab.com/multnomah-village-lucky-labrador-public-house

cky Lab Tap Room North
00 N Killingsworth Street
3-505-9511; luckylab.com/north-tap-room

BaseCamp Brewing
930 Southeast Oak Street
503.764.9152;
basecampbrewingco.com

Tidbit Food Farm & Garden
S.E. 28th Place and Division St.
foodcartsportland.com

Tin Shed Garden Café
1438 Northeast Alberta Street
tinshedgardencafe.com

Lovejoy Bakers
939 Northwest 10th Avenue
503.208.3113; lovejoybakers.com

Green Dog Pet Supply
4327 NE Fremont Street
503.528.1800
greendogpetsupply.com

Chimney Park
9360 N Columbia Boulevard
portlandoregon.gov/parks

Tryon Creek State Park
11321 SW Terwilliger Blvd
tryonfriends.org

Hotel Rose
50 SW Morrison Street
503.221.0711
staypineapple.com

Sentinel Hotel
614 Southwest 11th Avenue
03.224.3400; sentinelhotel.com

Jupiter Hotel
800 E. Burnside Street
503.230.9200; jupiterhotel.com

Mount Tabor Park

Portland Dog Parks

FENCED SITES

Brentwood Park
SE 60th Avenue and Duke

Chimney Park
9360 N Columbia Blvd

Delta Park
N Denver Avenue and MLK, Jr Blvd

The Fields
NW 11th Avenue and Overton Street

Gabriel Park
SW 45th Avenue and Vermont Street

Luuwit View Park
NE 127th Avenue and Fremont Street

Lynchwood Park
SE 170th Avenue and Haig Street

Normandale Park
NE 57th Avenue and Halsey Street

Sacajawea Park
NE 75th Avenue and Alberta Street

Wallace Park
NW 25th Avenue and Raleigh

UNFENCED SITES

Arbor Lodge Park
N Bryant Street and Delaware Avenue

Cathedral Park
N Edison Street and Pittsburg Avenue

Overlook Park
N Fremont Street and Interstate Avenue

Portland International Raceway
N Denver Avenue and Victory Blvd

Photo by Nichole Sears

Couch Park

lberta Park
E 22nd Avenue and Killingsworth Street

rgay Park
E 141st Avenue and Failing Street

ast Holladay Park
E 130th Avenue and Wasco Street

ernhill Park
E 37th Avenue and Ainsworth Street

azer Park
E 52nd Avenue and Hassalo Street

rant Park
E 33rd Avenue and U.S. Grant Place

ving Park
E 7th Avenue and Fremont Street

ilshire Park
E 33rd Avenue and Skidmore Street

ouch Park
W 19th Avenue and Glisan Street

herry Park
E 110th Avenue and Stephens Street

Creston Park
SE 44th Avenue and Powell Blvd

Laurelhurst Park
SE 39th Avenue and Stark Street

Lents Park
SE 92nd Avenue and Holgate Street

Mt. Tabor Park (partially fenced)
SE Lincoln Street, east of SE 64th Avenue

Sellwood Riverfront Park
SE Spokane Street and Oaks Pkwy

Sewallcrest Park
SE 31st Avenue and Market Street

Woodstock Park
SE 47th Avenue and Steele Street

Council Crest Park
SW Council Crest Drive

Hillsdale Park
SW 27th Avenue and Hillsdale Hwy

Willamette Park
SW Macadam Avenue and Nebraska Street

Oregon Wine Country

THERE'S MORE TO OREGON WINE COUNTRY THAN WHAT'S IN THE GLASS...A LOT MORE.

Oregon is known for its wine and love of dogs, so what could be more natural than taking your dog on a three-day road trip to dog-friendly wineries? Your pup can't be your designated driver, but you'll still enjoy sipping a glass of wine, gazing out at the exquisite landscape with Bowzer by your side.

Known for its pinot noir, the Willamette Valley was named 2016 Wine Region of the Year by Wine Enthusiast Magazine. Over two-thirds of Oregon's wineries and vineyards are in this region, totaling nearly 500. Other cool-climate varietals grown here include pinot gris, pinot blanc, chardonnay, riesling and gewürztraminer.

STAY Spend the night at the dog-friendly **Best Western Plus Rivershore Hotel** in Oregon City. Start your day with breakfast at the hotel's Rivershore Restaurant, where you can look out on fishing boats floating by on the Willamette River. After breakfast, go for a quick walk on the riverfront path behind the hotel to burn off some energy before the day's activities. Then it's a short hop to your next destination: the nearby marina for a morning kayak trip.

After a quick safety and paddling lesson from Sam Drevo of **eNRG Kayaking,** you're off

Clockwise from top: Sam Drevo of eNRG Kayaking leads a tour with his dog Mojo; Nandi at Wooden Shoe Tulip Farm; the chickens have come home to roost at Springhill Cellars in Albany; Whiskey Hills Winery's '15 rosé is made entirely with grapes from their farm.

GETTING HERE From Portland, take on I-5 S to OR-34 W in Linn County. Follow OR-34 W to NW 4th St/Pacific Hwy W in Corvallis or Hwy 20 E/Santiam Hwy SE in Lebanon.

a tandem kayak for a guided
ur of Willamette Falls and other
ver landmarks. Human gear is
ovided, but don't forget to bring
life jacket for your dog. Drevo's
lden mix, Mojo, who might join
ou for the trip, has seen it all
fore and barely lifts his head up
om resting on the kayak to bark
ck at the barking sea lions. As
revo dispenses historical tidbits
out the river, Oregon City and
e paper mill, catch glimpses of
urgeon jumping out of the water
d ospreys circling overhead.
revo recommends kayaking only
r small and medium-sized dogs.
gger dogs run the risk of tipping
e kayak over.

After the 90-minute tour, head
the dog-friendly covered patio
McMenamins Old Church &
Jb in Wilsonville for lunch. They
rve Northwest-style pub fare
ith locally and regionally-sourced
gredients. Their Cajun tots come
ghly recommended.

Next, drive out to family-run
Whiskey Hill Winery in Canby and
y the white pinot noir for which
ey're known. The winery has its
igins in a land-use technicality.
heir farm couldn't get a permit
host events—but a winery
ith 15 acres of pinot noir grapes
uld. Winemaker Chris Helbling's
ackground is in exercise science,
ut he's delved into the art of wine
aking. Dogs aren't allowed in the
sting room but are welcome at the
overed, outdoor patio.

Next, be sure to visit the **Wooden
hoe Tulip Farm** in Woodburn.
troll the tulip fields to admire
e bright spots of color (when in
loom), then make your way to the

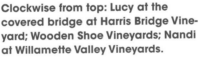

Clockwise from top: Lucy at the covered bridge at Harris Bridge Vineyard; Wooden Shoe Vineyards; Nandi at Willamette Valley Vineyards.

Photos by Lindsay Bacca

tasting room. Admission to the tulip festival held here each spring includes two free tastes of wine. Their sparkling blush moscato has won awards, but it's the Marechal Foch that tasting room worker Gina introduces to visitors as her "tall, dark and handsome" boyfriend. The farm also offers tours on a wine wagon that dogs can join. Leashed dogs are welcome in the indoor tasting room as well as the tulip fields. The farm occasionally hosts fundraisers and other events for dog rescues, as well.

At **Willamette Valley Vineyards**, enjoy stunning views while sipping a pinot on their expansive deck. On a sunny day, their lush lawn makes the perfect place for a picnic with your pup. Founded in 1983 by Oregon native Jim Bernau with the dream of creating world-class Pinot Noir, Willamette Valley Vineyards has grown from a bold idea into one of the region's leading wineries, earning the title "One of America's Great Pinot Noir Producers" from Wine Enthusiast Magazine.

Photos by Lindsay Bacca

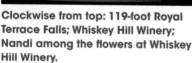

Clockwise from top: 119-foot Royal Terrace Falls; Whiskey Hill Winery; Nandi among the flowers at Whiskey Hill Winery.

PLAY A trip to the region would not be complete without a visit to **McDowell Creek Falls County Park** in Lebanon. The Falls Loop hike is an easy outing offering an array of waterfalls. Eearly in the season, the falls are a steady column of water instead of a trickle.

After a hike, it's back to wine tasting and **Springhill Cellars** in Albany. The family-run winery's best-seller is their Mer Vin pinot noir. Enjoy a taste in their indoor tasting room, which is dog-friendly, as is the patio. The winery has won numerous awards for its pinot noir, and puts a premium on being eco-friendly and sustainable by dry farming (not using an irrigation system) and planting cover crops.

Over at **Harris Bridge Vineyard** in Philomath, they specialize in dessert wines, aperitifs and vermouth made with pinot gris and pinot noir grapes. Their wine club is called Ivy's Axe, so named after a town prohibitionist

in the 1900s who chopped up illicit moonshine barrels with her axe. Some of the bottles come with short stories written by the former resident vineyard writer. The vineyard dog, Cork, a two-year-old Chihuahua, might accompany you on a stroll around the vineyard that takes you over the covered bridge, past the river and summer swimming hole and to a place to picnic under the oak trees. It's a gathering spot for the community. Dogs are allowed on the covered, outdoor patio as well as the indoor tasting room.

SIT On a sunny weekday night at **Block 15 Brewery and Tap Room** in Corvallis, it's the perfect place to hang out. Block 15 offers a variety of craft styles including ale, lagers, stouts, and wilds and sours. Dogs are allowed on the patio.

Afterward, watch the sunset from the riverfront walking path behind the **Holiday Inn Express** and help yourselves to freshly baked cookies and milk set out daily for people with late night snack cravings.

In the morning, a walk on the riverfront leads to **Tried & True Coffee** in downtown Corvallis. They serve coffee from their sibling company, Bespoken Coffee Roasters, and lattes here are artfully poured. Dogs are allowed on the outdoor patio if you can find a spot, but there are only three small tables. Returning to the nearby riverwalk offers more seating options.

Wilsonville Old Church & Pub
30340 S.W. Boones Ferry Rd, Wilsonville
503.427.2500; mcmenamins.com

Whiskey Hill Winery
29510 S Barlow Rod, Canby
503.974.7143; whiskeyhillwinery.com

Wooden Shoe Vineyards
33814 S Meridian Road; Woodburn
503.634.2243; woodenshoe.com

Willamette Valley Vineyards
8800 Enchanted Way SE, Turner
503.588.9463; wvv.com

McDowell Creek County Park
43170 McDowell Creek Drive, Lebanon
linnparks.com/parks

Springhill Cellars
2920 NW Scenic Drive, Albany
541.928.1009; springhillcellarswinery.com

Cardwell Hill Winery
24241 Cardwell Hill Drive, Philomath
541.929.9463; cardwellhillwine.com

Harris Bridge Vineyard
22937 Harris Road, Philomath
541.929.3053; harrisbridgevineyard.com

Block 15 Brewery & Tap Room
3415 SW Deschutes Street, Corvallis
541-752.BEER; block15.com

Tried & True Coffee
160 SW Madison Avenue, Corvallis
503.510.7010; triedandtruecoffee.co

Gathering Together Farm
25159 Grange Hall Road, Philomath
541.929.4270; gatheringtogetherfarm.com

PLAY The next stop is **Peavy Arboretum**, which is operated by Oregon State University and free to the public. Dogs are allowed to be off leash if under voice control. It's a shared forest, so watch out for logging trucks, cyclists, horses and wildlife.

If you're looking for a special meal, **Gathering Together Farm's Farmstand** in Philomath is a cozy farm-to-table restaurant focused on highlighting its produce. The 50-acre farm grows over 50 different types of vegetables. Featuring Italian peasant cuisine, the seasonal menu changes often. Dogs are not allowed indoors or on the patio, so find a reliable pet sitter if you wish to partake. 🐾

Top: Lucy at Harris Bridge Vineyards which specializes in dessert wines; Nandi at McDowell Creek Falls County Park.

ORE INFORMATION

st Western Rivershore Hotel
00 Clackamette Drive, Oregon City
3.655.7141; bestwesternoregon.com

oliday Inn Express On the River
1 NE 2nd Street, Corvallis
0.340.4291; hiexpress.com

Phoenix Inn and Suites
3410 Spicer Drive SE, Albany
541.926.5696; phoenixinn.com

eNRG Kayaking
1701 Clackamette Dr
Oregon City; 503.772.1122
enrgkayaking.com

Photos by Lindsay Bacca

Oregon Coas

RUGGED COASTLINE, CRASHING
WAVES, CANINE COMPANIONS...
THE OREGON COAST IS CALLING.

Oregon's rugged coastline and
quaint beach towns are just 90 min
utes from downtown Portland and
along the main stretch from Astori
to Newport, you will find your
pooch is welcome with open paws

STAY In Astoria, the **Cannery Pier
Hotel** throws out the welcome ma
for mutts with an oversized doggy
bed, food and water bowls, and a
basket generously filled with treat
bottled water and baggies.

In Newport (and Cannon Beach)
Hallmark Oceanfront Resorts
provides its four-legged guests
with their own sheet and towel for
wiping off sandy paws, custom
water bottle and bowl for trips to
the beach, frisbee throw toy, poope
scoopers and doggie cookies.

The **Surfsand Resort** in Cannon
Beach provides dogs with a comfy
pet bed, towel, sheet, placemat,
and food and water bowls. In the
lobby, Fred's Cookie Jar—named i
honor of a beloved resort mascot—
always filled with tasty dog treats,
and Fred's Foot and Paw Wash
is conveniently located near the
beachfront path, so you can wash
off sandy feet and paws. Speaking
of beach, the Surfsand sits perched
on the Pacific and is just steps from
Cannon Beach's world-famous land
mark, **Haystock Rock**. Accessible b
foot at low tide, Haystock Rock rise
235 feet high and is surrounded by

**Clockwise from top: Blaze at the beach in Lincoln City; beach access
at SurfSand Resort; Thya at SurfSand; Ecola State Park; Haystock Rock.**

GETTING HERE From Portland, take
US-26 and merge onto Hwy-101 S.

de pools—home to many critters including starfish, sea anemone, abs, chitons, limpets, and sea ugs. The rock is also a nesting te for many sea birds, including rns and puffins.

LAY Oregon beaches are super og friendly and most allow dogs be off leash as long as they are nder voice control. And, the mild mperatures make it an ideal estination any time of year.

In addition to Haystock Rock, visit to Cannon Beach would ot be complete without a stop at **cola State Park**. Ecola State Park a hiking and sightseeing mecca, ith trails situated above nine iles of Pacific Ocean shoreline. isitors to the park are treated to liffside viewpoints overlooking cture-perfect seascapes—pull up blanket on the grass or grab one f the picnic tables and settle in for leisurely afternoon.

If you find you are running low n dog supplies, stock up at **Dogs llowed**, a destination for dogs nd dog lovers, with organic food nd treats plus toys and accesso- es as well as a variety of Oregon- ade goods such as collars by Portland's Cycle Dogs and gear from Bend's wn Ruffwear.

Equally charming, the town of Newport is home to **Yaquina Head Light- ouse** and **Nye Beach** where you can walk miles of sandy shoreline and visit n array of quaint shops, restaurants and coffee houses. Be sure to stop in at lana's **Irish Pub**, with a pet friendly patio where you can enjoy a delicious owl of their signature clam chowder.

IT Located a few blocks away is **Café Stephanie**. You can smell the omemade quiche from down the street and there is ample outside seating, o grab breakfast or coffee with your four legged friend. Plus—they serve verything from omelets to giant homemade cinnamon rolls!

Next, head to historic Nye Beach, a favorite recreational area for more han 100 years. Just a five minute drive from Nye Beach is the **Yaquina Bay**

Clockwise from top: Enjoying the stunning views at Ecola State Park; Thya at the beach near SurfSand Resort; Blaze among the driftwood.

Driftwood photo by Lindsay Bacca; others by Julie Clegg

Bridge—a spectacular sight. Head over the pedestrian friendly bridge to take some pictures and admire the fishing boats passing underneath. This is one of the best attractions in all of Newport!

STAY After watching the sunset, check into your hotel—we recom- mend the lovely **Hallmark Resort Newport**, where you will receive a welcome doggie bag, with a note from Bailey—the Hallmark's resident beagle. The doggie bag

Clockwise from top: Bruiser enjoys a romp on the beach; Hallmark Resort in Newport; Bruiser in Newport.

Photos by Lindsay Bacca

Finish the evening with a stroll along the Pacific. The less than five minute walk from your room to the beach is one of the hotel's finest features for two- and four-legged alike.

Another fine feature? Hallmark Resorts donates a portion of the pet fee ($20 per pet) to local shelters. In 2015, they donated $10,00 to the Lincoln County Animal Shelter in Newport and the Clatsop County Animal Shelter i Cannon Beach.

A trip to the Oregon Coast wouldn't be complete without at least a couple of days in **Lincoln City**. Driving north from Newport, one of the first things you will notice is the huge amount of driftwood lining the beaches of gorgeous Siletz Bay. Between October and May, Lincoln City's "Float Fairies" leave hand blown glass balls for beach goers to find amongst the driftwood.

The town has also been voted best place for kite flying in North America. Every June and October they host kite festivals that people flock to, and it's a mesmerizing sight. However, the beach is amazing any time of year and with seven and a half miles of gorgeous shoreline, there is always a great spot to relax and watch Fido frolic in the water.

STAY There are a plethora of pet friendly hotels in Lincoln City, but our favorite is the **Looking Glass** located in the historic Taft district and just steps away from the beach. The Looking Glass not only welcomes pups with open arms and big smiles, but also ensures

includes a pet sheet for the bed, pet towel for sandy paws, yummy biscuits, poop bags, a Frisbee and pawesome water bowl for thirsty pooches. The property also features two pet areas—one is on the south end (oceanside) and the other overlooks the bluff by the north beach steps. Both areas feature wash down stations for sandy paws and salty fur.

While the Hallmark certainly pampers its pooches, it also pampers its people. The rooms are generously sized, with a king size bed, gas fireplace, in-room spa tub and kitchenette. Amenities include a microwave, refrigerator and locally-roasted Thundermuck Coffee plus WiFi and DVD rentals. Best of all, there's a view from every room.

SIT If you have a hankering for Dungeness crab (you are in the Dungeness capital of the world, afterall), **Georgie's Beachside Grill** is right next door and will deliver to your patio. Or, consider a picnic on the beach.

eir stay is just as great as yours. In ur room, you will find a welcome sket for Bowzer, complete with od and water bowls, treats, poop gs and towels. The Inn also has a ace to rinse sandy paws after your ach adventure plus a designated t area for the rest of your pet's eds. Be sure to check out the oto album in the lobby featuring ppy dog visitors—it's so sweet. It's onderful to have a place where the hole family feels welcome.

T After a whole lot of fun explor-g the beach, head out to find more t friendly places, starting with ki's. It's the best place in town to njoy delicious chowder, ahi tacos or foot-long hot dog. They even bring ur dog treats, too! With whimsical écor and cool rock music playing, ang out on the covered porch (per-ct for any weather) to sip mojitos nd plan your next adventure.

Start with a visit to the **Salty Dog ound Lounge** to drop off Fido for me play time with furry friends hile you explore the shops in incoln City. You can also arrange have him groomed.

With art galleries, boutiques, ntique shops and designer outlets, here is no shortage of shopping in incoln City. One of our favorites is **rehistoric**, where you can find fos-ls, minerals and meteorites. After a w hours of shopping, return to the lty Dog to find a happy and tired og, smelling fresh as a daisy for the ar ride home.

On your way out of town, swing y **Mojo Coffee** for a quick pick-me-p before the two-hour drive back Portland. Speaking of Portland, lojo serves hometown favorite, umptown Coffee! 🐾

MORE INFORMATION

Hallmark Oceanfront Resorts
1400 S Hemlock St., Cannon Beach
503.4361566; hallmarkinns.com

Surfsand Resort
148 W Gower Ave., Cannon Beach
503.436.2274; surfsand.com

Dogs Allowed
148-B N Hemlock St., Cannon Beach
dogsallowedcannonbeach.com

Hallmark Resort Newport
744 SW Elizabeth Street, Newport
855.391.2484; hallmarkinns.com

The Looking Glass Inn
861 SW 51st Street, Lincoln City
541.9963996; lookingglass-inn.com

Tiki's
1005 SW 51st Street, Lincoln City
541.996.4200

Salty Dog Hound Lounge
1345 SE 23rd Street, Lincoln City
541.996.7434; visitsaltydog.com

Mojo Coffee
3565 NW U.S. 101, Lincoln City
541.614.1800; mojocoffeeco.com

Photos by Lindsay Bacca

VISITOR INFORMATION

travelportland.com
visittheoregoncoast.com
traveloregon.com

Top: Tiki's serves up tasty treats on the pet-friendly patio. Above: Order a delicious cup o' Joe at Mojo in Lincoln City.

Mount Hood

TIMBERLINE LODGE OFFERS YOU AND FIDO MAGNIFICENT LODGING ON MOUNT HOOD.

Perched on the south slope of Mt. Hood at an elevation of 6,000 feet above sea level, **Timberline Lodge** is one of Oregon's most popular tourist attractions, drawing nearly two million visitors each year. This beautiful National Historic Landmark, dedicated in 1937 by President Franklin D. Roosevelt is, to this day, being used for its original intent—a magnificent ski lodge and mountain retreat for everyone to enjoy, including your four-legged friend.

STAY That's right, after close to 80 years, **Timberline Lodge** is now dog friendly, offering six pet-friendly rooms, decked out with all of the creature comforts your canine could ask for (if he could talk), including a comfy dog bed, food and water bowls, treats, his own Timberline Lodge bandana and of course, baggies for that all-important business. The rooms are rustic, yet comfortable—and most importantly, your canine can now crash with you after a long day's adventure.

PLAY Speaking of adventure, you and your hound are in mountain terrain and with that comes several trails for the two of you to explore, starting with **Mirror Lake Trail** and **Tom, Dick and Harry Mountain** (yes, that's really its name). This six mile trail has a 700-foot elevation change and once at the top, you and Fido are treated to one of the best alpine views in the National Forest.

Clockwise from top: Returning from a walk at Timberline Lodge; a sign in th elobby points out nearby peaks; Ginger relaxing on her bed provided by the lodge; the lodge's Cascade Dinging Room offers delicious cuisine; Louie sports his new Timberline bandana provided by the lodge.

GETTING HERE From Portland, follow I-84 E to Button Bridge Rd/Mt Hood Hwy in Hood River. Take exit 64 from I-84 E and follow OR-35 S to Cloud Cap Rd in Mount Hood.

Another trail with stunning views is **Burnt Lake**. This trail accesses the lake and Zigzag Mountain with views above the treeline. The north side also has wonderful old cedar snags showing remnants of a wildfire that came through around 1900. From the lake, there is a steep climb to Zigzag Mountain with views all around—Mt. Hood, Mt. Saint Helens, Mt. Rainier, Portland, and the Coast Range to name a few.

For a more leisurely time, **Wildwood Recreation Site** is a great place to enjoy a picnic with your pooch. Located along the Mount Hood Scenic Byway near the town of Welches, this day-use area is home to the Cascade Streamwatch Trail and Wildwood Wetlands Trail. The site offers plenty of picnic areas, playing fields, volleyball and basketball courts plus access to an extensive system of trails, where you and your pooch can explore natural stream and wetland ecosystems along accessible interpretive trails and boardwalks and observe native fish in an underwater fish-viewing chamber.

SIT Whether hiking to a mountaintop or enjoying a day at the park, you and your pooch have probably worked up an appetite. If so, then head straight to the pet-friendly patio at **Mt. Hood Brewing Company**, known as the brewery with an "altitude."

Mt. Hood Brewing produces tasty beer in small, hand-crafted batches with the highest quality ingredients available, including Mt. Hood glacier water. Not only that, it also serves up drool-wor-

Clockwise from top: The rooms are rustic, but comfortable; exploring the lodge; Timberline's Executive Chef Jason Stoller Smith.

Chef Stoller photo courtesy of Timberline; others by Lindsay Bacca

thy fare on its outdoor patio where dogs are welcome—so welcome in fact, dogs have their own special menu. While you cool off with a cold one, your canine companion can enjoy Frozen Yogurt Peanut Butter Balls (a perfect way to cool down your pooch after a long hike), Chicken and Rice Hash or Cheese Burger Patty. For you, start with the Pub Fry Poutine which includes a full pound of fries, peppercorn demi glace, fontina and fresh herbs. Or, the Deviled Eggs, topped with poppy seeds and crème fraîche. While your dog enjoys his Cheese Burger Patty, enjoy your own, on a bun, topped with Tillamook cheddar, lettuce, onion and a pickle.

The lobby is where guests hang out; St. Bernards have been a part of Timberline's tradition since 1937.

SIT Back at Timberline Lodge, enjoy a night cap or delicious cup of hot cocoa in the **Ram's Head Bar**, located on the second floor circular balcony surrounding the massive, 90-foot stone chimney and overlooking the lobby below. The bar also serves up a mean bowl of clam chowder, perfect after a day on the slopes. Speaking of slopes, Timberline Lodge offers the longest ski season in North America and is the only true ski-in and ski-out lodge in the state of Oregon.

If you want a more formal dining experience, the **Cascade Dining Room** offers a menu comprised of locally sourced ingredients including wild Pacific salmon as well as grass-fed beef from nearby ranches, located in the shadow of Mt. Hood. The lodge even sources its salt locally—hand harvested in Oregon by the Jacobsen Salt Company. With bellies full, enjoy a quiet night's sleep then start the next day with a swim at 6,000 feet! Yes, there is a heated outdoor swimming pool at Timberline Lodge—that, plus a hot tub—both open year round.

An amenity you and your pooch can both partake in is the outdoor patio and fire pit. Roast marshmallows, enjoy a glass of wine and relax in one of the Adirondack chairs with your best friend by your side.

For some down time, borrow a book from the lending library in the **Coyote's Den**. Or, enjoy a board game in one of the comfy seating areas surrounding the massive fireplace. Or, if you prefer to relax with your four-legged friend, upgrade your stay with wine, truffles, s'mores, cheese plate and more, delivered directly to your room.

While all good things must come to an end, keep an eye out for Bruno and Heidi behind the front desk when you check out. As the lodge's resident St.

Bernards, Bruno and Heidi are pleased to bid a happy farewell to you and your four-legged friend!

And, if you were still wondering—yes, Timberline Lodge is widely known as the hotel from Stanley Kubrick's movie The Shining, but there's nothing scary here. Warm, comfortable and inviting. Rich in Pacific Northwest history. Built by hand to withstand the ages. Oodles of charm and personality. And best of all, dog friendly—Timberline Lodge is truly a maginficent mountain getaway.

MORE INFORMATION
Timberline Lodge
27500 E Timberline Road
Timberline Lodge, Oregon
503.272.3311; timberlinelodge.com

Mt. Hood Brewing Company
87304 Government Camp Loop
Government Camp, Oregon
503.272.3172; mthoodbrewing.com

Acknowledgements

This guide is a culmination of 14 years of digging up the best places to sit, ay and play with your pooch in the Pacific Northwest. Since 2005, we have gged thousands of miles, traveling throughout Washington and Oregon (plus aho, Montana, Colorado, California and British Columbia) to find all that is do-friendly—and we could not do it without the writers and photographers ho have contributed to CityDog Magazine over the years including Julie ustin, Julie Clegg, Amelia Soper, Emily Rieman, Holly Cook, Jamie Pflughoeft, ri Pieper, Tushna Lehman, Jen Flynn, Nichole Sears, Lindsay Baca, April noi, Stephanie Olson, Brenda Bryan, Kate Hudson, Jessica Williams, Christine aplan, Val Mallinson, Kathleen Sorenson, Cathy Herholdt, Elizabeth and avid Henkes, managing editor Rebecca Sanchez, and assistant editor Susan enderson. This guide is also a result of all of our supporters below:

Merlin

ARLY SUPPORTERS San Juan Islands Visitors Bureau, Kendal Formo, Kathy Sorensen, Anne Saad, Laura Revesz, nda Donewald, Sharon Gray, Debbie Gallomore, Heidi Stromsoe, Lori Jean Paulino, Clifford Moore, Diana Kim, orrine Willhite, Vikki Bayman, Jim Litz, Christie White, Kay Hansen, Teresa Pliskowski, Robert Pregulman, ngie Ketelhut, Jen Silva, Karin Mellskog, Northwest Cellars Winery, Lodi and Lewi, Robin Honbo, Marilyn nbree, Sandy and Joe Wagele, John Knuth, Stig Serna, Stephanie Olson, Virginia Chapson, Sue Bell, Connie edmond, Lindsay Baca, The Rhoads Family, Julie Austin and Tina Pegar.

Bauer

BIG DOG SUPPORTERS Klaudina Pasko and Fenrir, Omar and Luz Lopez and Benz, Shelley Barouh and BellaRose, Sharon Gray, Savannah and Cooper, Olivia Heeter and Stella, Lori Nitchals and Mija, Linda Betts and Shani, Holly Cook and Mozi, Sherry Douceur and Radar, Cheri Evenson and Luci, Natalie Bachicha-Wells and Snoop Dogg, and Ellen Thomson and Honey.

TOP DOG SUPPORTERS (doggy photos on following pages) Breck Kane and Killian and Freckles, Shawnna Hodges and Ava and Rex, Matt and Annette Jones and Tuffy and Minnie, Mike and Fiona Fung and @ PorthosThePup, Anne and Bryce Kerker and Nellie and Brody, Bruce and Valerie Cronquist and Gracie Rose, aron LaVigne and Pebbles, Teena Kracht and Scout, Brenda Anderson and Gus Muppet, Lynn Caragol and my and Frankie, Cathie Coulter and Addie, George Torres and Erin Sanders and Bauer (left), Mookie Kaushal d Bindu Rathod and Birbal and Falkor, Diane Allerdice and Merlin (above), Jaci Hendricks and Louie the Jerk, m Coletti and Seamus, Susan Anda and Reuben, Mari Whitaker and Mimi, Joyce Juntunen and Dave Warren.

Keeping Current

While our informaiton is as current as possible, changes to pet policies, fees, regulations, parks, roads, and trails e made after we go to press. Businesses can close, change ownership or change their rules. Before you and your g begin your travels please be certain to call the phone numbers or visit the websites of the businesses listed in is book. And, if you find something that is incorrect please let us know at doggoneguide@citydogmagazine.com.

Addie

Scout

Gus Muppet

Pebbles

Louie the Jerk

Reuben

Birbal and Falkor

Mimi

Remy & Frankie

Killian & Freckles

Ava

@PorthosThePup

Rex

Brody

Tuffy & Minnie

Gracie Rose

Nellie

Seamus

Fetch More From CityDog Magazine

◀ SUBSCRIBE TO CITYDOG MAGAZINE

Smart, city-savvy and fun, CityDog Magazine brings the joys of life and living with dogs in the Pacific Northwest — from the city of Seattle to the Oregon Coast to Washington wine country — and everywhere in between. Subscribe today at citydogmagazine.com.

DOGGONE GUIDE TO SEATTLE+PUGET SOUND ▶

Coming in 2020...featuring a dog's eye view of your favorite neighborhoods, from funky Fremont to quirky Georgetown to downtown Seattle and beyond...this Doggone Guide is packed with the best places to sit, stay and play in the city you love with the four-legged love of your life. Want to grab a pint with your pooch? Check. Looking for a local dog park? Check. Want to meet fellow dog lovers at upcoming events? Check. Plus, hundreds of businesses and services that cater to your canine's every need!

◀ VISIT CITYDOGMAGAZINE.COM

We invite you to visit our website at citydogmagazine.com — you'll find digital editions of all of our past issues plus upcoming CityDog-hosted events like our CityDog Muttmixers and Cover Dog Model Search. Also, be sure to sign up for CityDog Unleashed, our monthly e-newsletter.

FOLLOW THE CITYDOG PACK

 facebook.com/ CityDogMagazine

 @citydogmagazine on Twitter

 @citydogmagazine on Instagram